T5-BBA-660

TAGASODE: WHOSE SLEEVES…

Kimono from the Kanebo Collection

TAGASODE: WHOSE SLEEVES…

Kimono from the Kanebo Collection

Nishimura Hyōbu
Jean Mailey
Joseph S. Hayes, Jr.

Japan Society, Inc.

(LUMA)
NK
8884
.A1
N57

The exhibition has been made possible in part by
a generous grant from Kanebo, Ltd.

TAGASODE : WHOSE SLEEVES...
Kimono from the Kanebo Collection
is the catalogue of the exhibition of Japan House Gallery
shown in the spring of 1976 as an activity of
Japan Society, Inc.

Copyright © 1976 by Japan Society, Inc.
Printed in Japan
Library of Congress Catalogue Card Number 75-37361
ISBN 0-913304-06-9

CONTENTS

FOREWORD

Among the textiles of ancient and medieval times, long before the age of science, are found woven and embroidered works of skill and subtlety unattainable by machine, as well as dyeing methods which modern knowledge is still unable fully to explain. Particularly in their design there are many examples of great artistry, with originality beyond the bounds of our modern imagination and freedom of expression fully reflecting the uncomplicated life of earlier times.

The textiles of each age possess a truly individual and alluring beauty and style, rooted in the life and technical skills of their time. Such precious materials, as representatives of their own ages and cultures, are truly treasures of mankind.

For many years now our company has been diligently collecting traditional textiles from each country of the world, prizing them as materials for the study of fabrics and fashion. In displaying some of these materials in the present exhibition it is our hope to contribute to cultural exchange between our two countries.

The kimono here displayed are kosode of the Edo period, specially selected from among the Japanese textiles included in the Kanebo

Collection. These are not articles created for stage or ceremonial use; most are kimono of the type worn and loved by ladies of the urban propertied class of the time. They are supremely Japanese, and are exquisite works of textile art.

In earlier days textile materials—sometimes elegant and refined, sometimes lushly and startlingly beautiful—were introduced together with superb technical skills from the lands of the west and south over the desert Silk Road of ancient and medieval times and the oceanic Silk Road of more recent centuries.

As a result the weaving and dyeing achievements of Japan, eastern terminus of the Silk Road, progressed rapidly to the point where Japan could pride itself in mastery of the quintessence of the traditional textile arts. Today it may be said that international exchange is flourishing even more broadly and smoothly over the Silk Road of the air.

We are most pleased on this occasion to have the opportunity to display these articles of traditional Japanese textile art to an American audience.

We shall be more than gratified if we have succeeded in contributing, through cultural history, to the deepening of friendship and understanding between the United States and Japan.

I would like to express our deep thanks to Professor Nishimura Hyōbu, Director of the Osaka Municipal Museum of Art, and Miss Jean Mailey, Curator of the Textile Study Room of The Metropolitan Museum of Art, for their expert assistance in the preparation of this catalogue; to the Japan Society for its unstinted support in sponsorship of the exhibition; and to Mr. Rand Castile, Director of Japan House Gallery, and his capable staff for their cooperation in this project.

Itoh Junji
President
Kanebo, Ltd.

ACKNOWLEDGMENTS

Tagasode ni
Kimi kasanuran
Karagoromo
Yonayona ware ni
Katashikasetsutsu

Whose sleeves do you enfold
While leaving me to lie here
Night after night
Alone on my widest robe?

Lady Sagami's verse is but one of the many in the early anthologies of Japan including *tagasode*. Whose sleeves... This evocative phrase—filled with fragrance and romance—is used here as the title for an exhibition of kimono, and serves to conjure the beautiful women who wore them and the aura surrounding them in Edo Japan. Since, alas, we cannot document the women who wore these splendors, we must content ourselves with discussions of details of workmanship and design. This, too, is rewarding for seldom in the history of national costumes has there been a dress so exquisite in color, ornament, and craftsmanship.

The Kanebo Collection numbers some eleven thousand items, and we have selected but forty-three kimono from this total to represent the Edo period, 1615-1868. The Collection is superb, and the examples presented here—including a number formerly in the famed Nagao Collection—cover virtually the entire range of techniques and style of the Edo kimono artists.

We are most fortunate in having as a Visiting Curator and author of the catalogue Prof. Nishimura Hyōbu,* Director of the Osaka Municipal Museum. It has been a pleasure to work with this distinguished authority on textiles of the Kanebo Collection. Working with him—and richly deserving of our thanks and praise was Mr. Joseph S.

Hayes, Jr., a representative in New York of Kanebo, Ltd., and an accomplished scholar in Japanese and Chinese. Mr. Hayes translated and adapted the catalogue as well as authored the exhaustive glossary. We are most appreciative of his unceasing labor on behalf of the exhibition and catalogue.

An early and avid supporter of the exhibition was Mr. Itoh Junji, acting Chairman of the Board and President, Kanebo, Ltd. and Kanebo Textile, Ltd. Mr. Itoh as chief officer of one of Japan's leading corporations encouraged us at every step of this project and made available a substantial corporate grant to the exhibition and catalogue. Our sincere thanks for this and Kanebo's generous loan of kimono.

His associate Mr. Sano Masao, Managing Director of Kanebo, Ltd. and Kanebo Textile, Ltd., made available the resources of the Fashion Institute of Kanebo in research of the myriad details of the collection. The International Department's Chief, Mr. Fukunaka Jūzo, handled most successfully the necessary negotiations for all phases of the exhibition. Working with Messrs. Sano and Fukunaka were their capable associates Mr. Yamashita Yoshio and Mr. Nakatsugawa Shōji.

The association of the Gallery and Kanebo has been a productive and exciting new venture for us.

Miss Jean Mailey, Curator, Textile Study Room, The Metropolitan Museum of Art, authored the introductory text of this catalogue as well as assisting with most valuable advice on all aspects of our first textile show. We knew Miss Mailey — for some time a member of the former art committee of the Society — and it was a pleasure to work anew with her.

We are indebted to many others; Dr. Miyeko Murase of Columbia University who was consulted frequently on this exhibition; Mr. Andrew Pekarik who provided a fine translation of the "*tagasode*" poem (above); Miss Kajitani Nobuko of The Metropolitan Museum of Art; Mrs. Maryell Semal, Miss Maekawa Mitsuko, and Mr. Imai Keiji of the Japan Society; and Mr. John Elliott, whose good offices helped advance this undertaking. To each a special thanks. And I would be remiss not to point out the splendid coordination of all phases of the kimono show by Ms. Margot Kneeland.

And may I also express personal thanks to the Gallery Chairman, Mrs. Jackson Burke, and to the Founders and Friends whose faithful support make these exhibitions possible.

Rand Castile, Director
Japan House Gallery

*All Japanese proper names are given in Japanese style, family name first, given name last.

AN INTRODUCTION TO
EDO KIMONO

The kimono of the Edo period represent a pinnacle in the long and colorful history of Japanese costume and the textiles associated with them. In these robes of 1615 to 1868, the costume and its free style ornament are conceived as a unit in a manner completely Japanese.

Vestiges and survivals from various stages of history that finally resulted in the Edo kimono go back to the 2nd century, when the Japanese emperor received a gift of silkworms from the emperor of Han China, a treasure made especially rich by the inclusion of the intricate lore of sericulture.

Japan benefited from her good fortune and, according to ancient records, produced three grades of silk and a great amount of the coarser bast fibers *(asa)*. In early times the bast fibers such as hemp were used by the poorer classes to weave material for their clothing.

The sheer forms of gauze, *ra* and *sha* (where groups of warps change position in relation to each other with each shed of the weaving, holding the wefts firmly in a spaced position), were introduced at an early period from China, too. *Sha* forms the ground of many summer robes of the Edo period (catalogue 21). Silk was worn by members of the court and used for taxes or income. Fabrics woven of ramie or hemp were worn by ordinary people until a 5th century emperor directed Korean immigrant weavers to make silk of more ordinary quality which might be worn by plain people. These examples, copied in the provinces, were the first efforts to popularize silk.

The 7th century rise to power of the Fujiwara family saw the establishment of the Imperial Weaving Bureau and the Guild of Needleworkers of the Ministry of the Imperial Household, as well as the Bureau of the Palace Wardrobe of the Ministry for Central Affairs.

Color, always a cult in Japan, was especially important in this period. Colors of hat cords were prescribed by edict to represent ranks of nobility, and perhaps to correspond to the Five Elements and Five Virtues: blue (wood, humanity); red (fire, politeness); yellow (earth, faith); white (metal, justice); black (water, wisdom). The purple of the highest rank signified the male and female principles of Chinese cosmology, the perfect harmony of yang and yin. Eventually the aristocracy developed some 690 ranks with specific color combinations. At the same time the length and width of a bolt of silk were established by imperial decree.

Records of the Heian period (794-1185) tell us of the colors worn appropriately by season: spring called for robes resembling the bloom of the plum and the cherry; summer robes were blushed with the colors of azalea and wistaria; for fall were chosen the rich hues of reddening maple leaves, bush clover, chrysanthemum, and bluebell; the solemn pine green and brown of leaves were deemed harmonious with winter snow. This was the period of large, many-layered kimono. A woman wore as many as twenty robes — one over the other — though the name for this costume (jūni-hitoe) indicates only twelve layers. The colored layers came to be standardized, and did not always mean a kimono layer but extra folds of color at sleeves, neck, and hem. Madder root and Indian safflower yielded the reds; the fashionable incense brown and dead leaf brown were made from seeds of cape jasmine and hawthorne; blue was made from mountain indigo.

The Kamakura period (1185-1392), with its spartan spirit, made dress simpler. In accounts of this time there is an increasing mention of kosode, the kimono as we know it today. Kosode, "small sleeves," hitherto hidden by over-kimono or worn in plainest form by commoners, became the standard for all. Over it women wore red *hakama*, full trousers. On formal occasions a trailing, richly decorated robe, *uchikake*, was worn from the shoulders. This, too, with its padded hem is still used today.

The Muromachi period (1392-1568) was an age of war and turmoil. Domestic industry and production being at a low ebb, most fine textiles — both those of especially restrained elegance, worn for the tea ceremony, and the opulent silks of the Nō costumes — were imported, in the main, from China. Since these expensive imports were insufficient to meet demand, the plain weave domestic silks were increasingly enhanced by hand-decorated processes. The simple lines and soft fabrics of the now fashionable kosode and the splendidly decorated *uchikake* were more sympathetic to hand decoration than the often heavily brocaded imported silks. The Muromachi craftsmen tried to imitate the ornament of the Chinese with woven gold and silver yarns and with impressed gold leaf. These techniques combined with embroidery became a popular replacement for the Chinese imports.

The Momoyama period (1568-1615) brought an upheaval in Japanese society, a growth in individualism, and the development of grand and decorative design. This was the beginning of the era of great decorators. Kosode was now worn by all, regardless of distinctions in age or class. The taste for free-style and asymmetrical ornament distinguishes this period, as it came to distinguish Japanese from Chinese arts.

In the late Muromachi and Momoyama period trade with Ming China was resumed on a large scale. Satin damask silk such as *rinzu*, with a woven design of key fretting and stylized floral motifs, was introduced from China and found immediate favor as a supple and easily worked medium for the new decorative techniques of the time. Many of the finest kosode of Momoyama and Early Edo were made from imported Chinese figured satin or from similar material subsequently perfected in Japan. The suitability and adaptability of these supple silks are well attested by their use in many of the kimono in this collection. The decorative techniques at this time included embroidery, often combined with gold foil, and *tsujigahana*, a combination of finely stitched tie-dye and exquisitely hand-inked details.

The Edo period, 1615-1868, was generally one of unprecedented prosperity and development, and particularly witnessed the expansion of flourishing town and city life.

Tokugawa Ieyasu, trusted counselor and general to Hideyoshi, was the first Tokugawa shogun, ruling lord. The Tokugawa shogunate continued in rule throughout this period. Hideyoshi, unifier and master of all Japan, had given Ieyasu Edo castle as the seat of his fiefdom and on the wild marshland surrounding it, Ieyasu built the city of Edo. This city was to become the capital of Japan now called Tokyo. Suspicious of foreigners and the international trade that Hideyoshi had encouraged, and fearful of external interference, the shogunate gradually imposed an almost complete ban on trade outside Japan. Simultaneously, there was launched a relentless persecution of Japanese converts to Christianity. The shogunate permitted only intermittent trade with the Dutch at Nagasaki, the Spanish in the Philippines, and with Siam, where a colony of Japanese Christians and followers of Hideyoshi was established. This isolation was enforced until 1853 when Commodore Perry's ships appeared at the entrance to Tokyo harbor. The two and a half centuries of nearly total isolation permitted Japan to develop a purely native cultural style.

The Tokugawa shogunate's policy of keeping the feudal lords weak and disunited resulted in the rise of a middle class to wealth, power, and educational privileges that previously had been the exclusive prerogative of the aristocracy and feudal overlords. Lively new arts and literature reflecting the life of the common people accompanied this rise. Through the *ukiyo-e*, "floating world," school of painting and woodblock prints, the minutely realistic novels of Saikaku, and the dramas of Chikamatsu, depicting this lifestyle, high culture became a possession and representation of the people.

The weaving industry continued in favor with the Tokugawa shogunate. New forms of polychrome patterned weaving developed. Important now was hand decoration of the robes made of soft monochrome crepes, figured satin, and the crisper gauzes produced for this purpose mainly in Nishijin, the northwestern area of Kyoto still famed for silk production. This free-style decoration reflected the ever increasing independence of Japanese design from Chinese or other foreign influences.

The first great Japanese free-style kosode are those of Early Edo, foreshadowed in Late Momoyama, with the kimono divided into asymmetrical areas of black, orange, and white, with details in embroidery, imprinted gold, and tie-dye. These are the Keichō *somewake* kimono, the particolor style developed in the Keichō era 1596-1615, (catalogue 2).

Another great free-form style can be seen in the bold, simple unerringly composed ornament of the robes of the Kambun era (1661-1673) as seen here in catalogue 3, 4, 5. Tie-dye, where large shapes were outlined with fine stitchery drawn tight, was often combined with finely knotted tie-dye *(hitta)* and with embroidery and impressed or couched gold detail. The details here were typically stylized from various aspects of the chrysanthemum; see cover detail and catalogue 3. This kind of design, strategically

complemented by large undecorated areas, was made necessary by two great fires; one in Edo in 1657, and one in Kyoto in 1661. So many people lost all their belongings that innumerable new robes were required at once. A robe decoration concentrating difficult technical efforts in smaller areas — using generous amounts of negative space in the design — made a large production possible. It is significant that one of Japan's finest kimono design styles quickly resulted. These designs are recorded in the first Japanese fashion catalogues *(hiinagata)* in which each design is wood blocked in black and white, one to a page.

As the Edo period advanced, subjects were rendered in delicate, naturalistic form in the poetic mood of the Kanō school of painting. Tie-dye and painted detail, with embroidery and impressed gold and silver, were used for these new forms. Two or more gold threads were now couched down in outlines where one previously had been used. Sometimes a whole flower or leaf was worked in couched gold thread. In silk the direction stitch or satin stitch was used for flowers, cranes, tortoises, and other natural objects. Long float stitches with couching in geometric or naturalistic patterns were often used for inanimate objects, treasures, and symbols. In a typical treatment of a leaf the central vein was formed by long embroidery stitches. The ground fabric on either side of this suggests the radiating side veins. This was thought to resemble hands raised in prayer.

An extensive use of finely knotted tie-dye was employed for the most precious robes of the Edo period. This tie-dye technique called *hitta* was used in a variety of ways to define selected areas of the design. A version with only the linear outlines of the decoration left untied was called *sō-hitta*; *sō* in this case implies a covering of the entire surface. This technique was done free hand, with hundreds of thousands of knots as close together as possible and tied over silver nails. The fabric was dipped in water containing straw ash to set the dye and tighten knots, then dipped in the dye bath. The knots were removed with small silver scissors. The relief surface is part of the charm of this extraordinary treatment, usually done on plain-weave silk or figured satin (catalogues 25-28).

Stories of the Empō era (1673-1681) illustrate the important part beautiful robes played in the life of all levels of society. Wealthy merchants' wives went to great lengths to surpass each other. At picnics in Ueno Park samurai parties were sheltered behind curtains with family crests. Others happily made impromptu curtains by stretching cords from trees and hanging their festive wraps and over-kimono from them — a prospect as beautiful as flowers themselves, according to a report of the day. The *tagasode* ("whose sleeves...") screens of the Momoyama period repeat this display in painted surfaces featuring kimono draped on stands or hung from silken cords. This effect was later reproduced on screens, using fragments of historic kimono, most notably of the outstanding Nomura collection now in Tokyo. The designs, usually unique, and often rendered in a

combination of techniques, were as innumerable as they were allusive: flowers and grasses of the four seasons; fans on the water (a reference to the "floating world"); wheels (a reference to the aristocracy); butterflies; gourds on a garden fence; scenes from literature; famous city views; and country or shore landscapes.

Mounting extravagances provoked a reaction. In the third year of Tenna, 1683, the first of many sumptuary edicts was promulgated. Gold brocades, embroidery, or overall finely knotted tie-dye were forbidden for robes. Increasingly stringent restrictions followed at short intervals. A great change in fashion and technique in robe decoration resulted. A stenciled imitation tie-dye, *suri-hitta*, replaced the exquisite hand knotted variety which had required such time and skill.

Kyoto's most popular and far-reaching contribution to the field of dyeing is the cloth dyed many colors by a method called *yūzen-zome*, named for the artist-designer associated with it. Yūzen, who lived in Kyoto for much of his life, was first known for his painted fans. He employed the old technique of resist-dye and the newer one of painting with dyes to meet the demands of the Genroku era (1688-1703) for bold and striking designs. The backgrounds of *yūzen* include wax-resist dye of 8th century silks and the wax-resist dye cottons of the 17th century *(sarasa)*. The latter technique was imported from India and southeast Asia through Thailand, and later made in Japan. Its most immediate antecedents lay in the paste-resist dye of Kaga province which was a wealthy and important center of artistic life and culture. The local rulers, the Maeda family, were for generations keen patrons of the arts.

Another type of resist-dye technique popular at the same time as *yūzen* was *chaya-tsuji,* named for the Chaya family of Kyoto whose specialty was free-hand decoration in indigo resist-dye on ramie (catalogue 14). Its designs showed the same fine linear detail as that seen in *yūzen.* The beautiful understated fabrics decorated in *chaya-tsuji* were reserved for the households of the rulers and never knew the popular success of *yūzen.*

Yūzen's great contemporary, the painter Ogata Kōrin (1658-1716), created significant works in many mediums and is known to have designed at least a few robes in the Tokyo National Museum and one with a large black pine tree, mentioned in a book published in 1699. A robe in this exhibition, painted in ink with a powdering of gold, catalogue 13, is attributed to him. This, however, may not be his, but after his style by an admiring follower.

Though embroidery, hand painting, and the application of gold foil continued in use, the development of decorative technique during Edo depended less on the discovery of new ways to apply color than on that of ways to prevent its application where unwanted: that is, on the development and perfection of resist techniques. Such techniques included both tie-dye methods such as drawn stitch tie-dye and very finely knotted tie-dye *(hitta),* as well as the starch-resist techniques *(yūzen, chaya-tsuji)* perfected in the early eighteenth century as a result in part of the sumptuary restriction of embroidery, gold foil, and overly elaborate tie-dye.

The 19th century saw further refinement of the now established techniques. Motifs continued in the classic vein developed over a period of more than a thousand years.

The increasing interest at this time in the obi and its subsequent enlargement played a significant role in the decoration of the kimono. The broad expanse of the large obi tended to divide the kimono surface into distinct upper and lower areas. This forced a new concept in overall design. Now designs were by and large confined to borders. Exceptions were the *uchikake,* over-kimono, worn without sash, and the furisode for young ladies and marriage robes.

Also influencing the design and weave of kimono were the sumptuary laws restricting elaborate and costly techniques. This made the designers and their clients more reserved, more subtle in their taste. Coupled with caution the Japanese love of the simple, fine, and understated created a restrained elegance perhaps best seen in the Late Edo kimono of this exhibition.

This mood continues in Japan today. The traditions have not been lost, and while kimono of quality are increasingly rare and expensive, one can still glimpse in corners of Kyoto and Tokyo the beautiful sleeves that inspired this show.

Jean Mailey

Note:
I should like to offer special acknowledgment to the sensitive and sympathetic study of this subject by Helen Benton Minnich in collaboration with Shojiro Nomura in *Japanese Costume and the Makers of Its Elegant Tradition.*

PLATES AND CATALOGUE

1
KOSODE with plum and bamboo
Tie-dye *(nuishime-shibori and hitta)*
     with ink drawing and particolor
     dye *(somewake)*
Yellow and black particolor figured
     satin *(rinzu)*
Early Edo***   142.0 cm x 66.0 cm****

The kosode (literally, small sleeves) was the prototype of the kimono of today's Japan. Originally an undergarment of the classical Heian period, it was so named to distinguish it from the *ōsode* (large sleeves) which made up the then many outer layers of formal female attire. By contrast the kosode had only narrow hand openings at the ends of the sleeves. It is the narrowness of the opening — rather than the volume of the sleeve itself — which is the defining characteristic.

This kosode is dyed in two basic background colors: yellow and, in the left shoulder and right hem, a deep black. This use of more than one background color to define different areas of the design is known as *somewake* (dye-separation); in this example the different panels of the ground are marked off by pine-bark and cloud shaped borders.

On the black ground are shown plum branches and blossoms among falling frost; the plum blossoms are done in drawn-stitch tie-dye *(nuishime-shibori)*. On the yellow ground are depicted sprays of bamboo leaves in *hitta*, sometimes known as *kanoko*, a tie-dye resist technique using very small, regularly-spaced knots to fill in an area of the design. On one of the bamboo leaves a squirrel and grapes are drawn in by hand in India ink. The combined motif of squirrel and grapes enjoyed a great vogue in the Momoyama and Early Edo periods.[1]

In its composition and techniques this piece draws much from the *tsujigahana* style which flourished during the preceding Momoyama period, and which was based upon the combined use of tie-dye and hand painted detail.

*For purposes of this catalogue the Edo period has been divided into Early (through Genroku), Middle (through Kansei), and Late: divisions which happen to coincide roughly with the seventeenth, eighteenth, and nineteenth centuries.
**Dimensions show height from shoulder to hem and sleeve length from center back seam to hand opening.

18

2
**KOSODE with flowers, lozenges,
and clouds**
Tie-dye *(hitta)* **and particolor dye
*(somewake)***
**Crimson, white, and purple figured
satin** *(rinzu)*
Early Edo   147.0 cm x 59.0 cm

The design details of small blossoms, cloud patterns, and linked lozenges are brought out by tie-dye on a particolor figured satin ground. The major ground areas are defined by particolor dye and give the appearance of having been pieced together from separate scraps of crimson, white, and purple silk. Though the overall conception is bold, the details have been treated with simplicity, and the result is a coherent and satisfying design.

This piece is an example of the Keichō particolor *(somewake)* style which developed early in the seventeenth century. The Keichō era, 1596-1615, marked the transition between Momoyama and Edo, but neither the use of the term Keichō kosode nor the style itself was restricted to kimono made during the Keichō era. In contrast to the clearly developed and independently presented motifs of Momoyama, the Keichō style involved the combined use of heterogenous and often overlapping motifs filling the entire surface and usually achieved through the use of a variety of techniques on a particolor ground. In addition to tie-dye, embroidery and gold leaf applique *(surihaku)* were frequently employed in Keichō kosode, though these elements are absent here.

The particolor style itself is said to have been inspired by the Indian textiles *(sarasa)* first imported into Japan in the late sixteenth century.

3
**KOSODE with chrysanthemums and
    snowflake ring**
**Tie-dye (*hitta*), embroidery, and
    gold leaf (*surihaku*)**
White figured satin (*rinzu*)
Early Edo   145.0 cm x 61.5 cm

The material is a white figured satin woven with a large stylized floral pattern (*rangiku*) superimposed on key fretting (*saya-gata*). Featured in the design — which is conceived as extending leftward and downward from the right shoulder and sleeve — are prominent chrysanthemums interleaved with a large yellow snowflake ring (*yukiwa*; see Glossary). In contrast to the plain white of much of the left side, the right side is made even more splendid by bold vertical stripes.

The large chrysanthemums, snowflake ring, and light vertical stripes are rendered in fine tie-dye, while the darker stripes and intervals in the main design are richly embroidered with smaller representations of chrysanthemum, cherry, and other blossoms, and with symbols of good fortune and wealth (*takarazukushi*).

This kosode, with its bold, large-scale designs contrasting with a broad expanse of plain ground, is an excellent example of the style which originated in the Kambun era, 1661-1673, following disastrous fires which destroyed the wardrobes of much of Edo (Tokyo) in 1657 and of Kyoto in 1661. The rush for replacement is reflected in a new boldness of design. The design of this kosode when worn — the sheer white of the left side against the splendor of the right — must have been stunningly effective. This was further enhanced by the contrast of large tie-dyed patterns with colorfully embroidered details.

A final element to be noted is the gold leaf applied originally in a fine line along the margins of the vertical stripes. Compared to the embroidery and tie-dye, which are boldly and lavishly employed, the use of gold leaf is restrained — a clear departure from the techniques of earlier periods. Gold leaf had originally been used to evoke the splendor of Chinese brocades woven with gold yarns using techniques unknown in Japan, and became a prominent feature of elegant pre-Kambun designs. By the end of the 17th century, however, new techniques of embroidery and tie-dye of the supple *rinzu* figured satin had been developed to the point where the extensive use of gold leaf— artificial in flavor, stiffening in effect, and vulnerable to sumptuary regulation — was no longer necessary for richness and elegance of design.

4
KOSODE with design of chrysanthe-
mums on a bamboo trellis
Tie dye (*hitta* and *bōshi-shibori*),
embroidery, and hand painting
White satin (*nume*)
Early Edo   140.0 cm x 66.0 cm

This kosode is in the Kambun style, characterized by bold and dramatic design (see catalogue 31), but the overall effect here is of tranquility. This sophisticated design is from a bird's eye perspective, much as in Japanese hand-scrolls.

The flowers and some of the leaves of the chrysanthemums are done in light blue and red finely knotted tie-dye *(hitta)*. Finely drawn ink lines may be seen around the out-lines of the light blue blossoms; these are the tracings for the stitching carried out in preparation for tying.

The trellis has been painted in by hand and the remaining leaves are carried out by hat tie-dye *(bōshi-shibori)* with embroidered detail. The primary technique here, how-ever, is tie-dye, with a limited use of embroidery.

5
KOSODE with cockscombs
Tie-dye *(hitta)* **and embroidery**
Yellow figured satin *(rinzu)*
Early Edo   153.0 cm x 67.0 cm

This kosode has a ground of yellow *rinzu* with a woven pattern of key fretting *(saya)* and blossom medallions. The surface decoration is of cockscombs *(keitō; Celosia argentea cristata)* spreading upward from hem to shoulders. Like the preceding, catalogue 4, the techniques include tie-dye with limited use of embroidery.

Since this also is an example of the Kambun style, the design is unfettered and the colors strong; yet the overall expression is one of placid tranquility, suggesting that this kosode was made in a period of lessened excitement and intensity somewhat after the glorious years of Kambun.

6
FURISODE with bamboo arcs
   and mandarin oranges
Tie-dye (*hitta* and *mokume-shibori*)
   and embroidery
White satin (*shusu*)
Middle Edo   159.0 cm x 63.0 cm

The *furisode* (literally, swinging sleeves) is a type of kosode with sleeves which extend downward from the arms toward the waist. Despite the enlarged volume of the sleeves it is regarded as a variant of the kosode (small sleeves) because it retains the characteristic and defining narrow hand opening.

In this example the bold arcs of bamboo suggest a bamboo hedge or fence. The circular areas marked off by the bamboo are filled with wood-grain tie-dye (*mokume-shibori*) made by gathering the fabric with fine parallel rows of horizontal stitching, rather like shirring, and then dyeing with indigo over a brownish gold background.

Interlaced among the bamboo are fruit-laden mandarin orange (*tachibana; Citrus tachibana*) branches rising upward from the hem. The branches and some of the fruit are done in finely knotted tie-dye; the remainder of the fruit is depicted by embroidered outlining around undyed satin ground.

The rest of the design, including the leaves of both bamboo and orange, is embroidered using delicately shaded yarns and couched gold.

The subtleness of shading in the embroidery is characteristic of the Genroku period, 1688-1704. The remarkable richness of this embroidery, together with the lavish use of the comparatively rare wood-grain tie-dye technique and the scrupulous regularity of the finely knotted hitta tie-dye reflect skilled craftsmanship in the creation of a kimono for a young lady of high social standing. In this example the detailing is in fact excessively precise, and this over-conscientiousness of execution tends to reduce the expressiveness of the design.

The sleeves of this kimono are long for the middle Edo period, but the furisode style was not unknown in the seventeenth century and a garment of similar style is described in the works of the novelist and social commentator Saikaku, who died in 1693.[2]

7
KOSODE with double blossom cherry
Resist dye *(yūzen)* and embroidery
Yellow silk crepe *(chirimen)*
Middle Edo   147.0 cm x 62.0 cm

Double blossom cherry trees *(yaezakura)* in full bloom spread from the hem upward and outward onto the sleeves of this kosode. Among the many varieties of flowering cherry the *yaezakura* blooms profusely but later than other varieties, simultaneously with the appearance of new leaves.

The trunk, blossoms, and leaves are executed in starch-resist dye *(yūzen)*, supplemented with embroidery in couched gold and colored yarns. The variety of ways in which the blossoms are depicted is startling; particularly notable are the remarkable permutations in the embroidery of the individual petals.

The strict sumptuary law of the third year of Tenna, 1683, which banned the excessive use of gold, embroidery, and tie-dye, provided a new impetus for the development of alternative decorative techniques. The most important of the techniques which now emerged was *yūzen* dyeing, a combination of starch-resist and hand painting which flourished during the Genroku period, 1688-1704, and reached the peak of its development in the Middle Edo (for details, see Introduction and Glossary).

This kosode is an exquisite example from the period. The subtle variation of shading achieved here provides an outstanding illustration of the inherent vividness and flexibility of the vegetable dye-stuffs used: the chemical dyes of modern times afford a more limited and brasher palette.

The embroidered characters scattered across the sleeves and shoulders read: first, discern, and spring; and constitute an allusion to a poem included in the eleventh century anthology *Wakan rōeishū* (Collection of Japanese and Chinese Poems for Recitation).[3] In this passage the poet lyrically describes the sight of cherry petals scattered from the trees by the winds of spring.

> The blooms fly like brocade—
> how richly colored—
> woven by the breeze,
> not yet neatly folded.
> I first discern the skill of spring wind
> upon its loom;
> weaving not only colors...
> weaving fragrances.

8
**KOSODE with wild ginger against
   mountain lane and mist**
Resist-dye *(yūzen)* **and embroidery**
White figured satin *(rinzu)*
Middle Edo   149.0 cm x 62.0 cm

The vigor of the embroidered zig-zag "mountain lane" motif is softened by the misty outlines within which the motif is contained. The remainder of the surface is filled with resist-dyed and embroidered vines, leaves, and flowers of the wild ginger *(aoi)*, symbolic of the Tokugawa shoguns through association with the triple *aoi* leaves of the Tokugawa family crest.

Across the top of the kosode, on back and front, the phrases *Chōseiden* and *Shunjūtomu* are embroidered in couched gold, with each character further embellished and accented with a small butterfly medallion. *Chōseiden*, the "Hall of Long Life," was the name of a palace building in T'ang China, and is taken as a reference to the personal residence of the ruler. *Shunjūtomu* — literally, "Springs and autumns abound," — is a phrase of even greater antiquity and refers to the youth and expected longevity of the ruler.

The two phrases occur together in a verse from the *Wakan rōeishū:*

> Within the Hall of Long Life
>   Springs and autumns abound.
> Before the Gate of Lasting Youth
>   Sun and moon slow down.[4]

The poem, one of congratulation, expresses the wish for a long life for the ruler; here it is linked by the wild ginger with the family crest of the Tokugawa. The theme of this design, therefore, is a celebration of the prosperity of the Tokugawa shoguns and the hope for their continuation.

This is an elegant and refined costume for a young lady.

9
KOSODE with checks and falcons,
   autumn maples, and waterfalls
Resist-dye *(yūzen)* **and embroidery**
Yellow silk crepe *(chirimen)*
Middle Edo   140.0 cm x 60.0 cm

The design of this kosode is clearly divided into upper and lower portions, reflecting the increasing importance of the widening obi in costume design from this time forward.

The upper portion of the garment is completely filled with a regular pattern of brown checks. Checks enjoyed a great vogue in the Middle Edo period after revival of the pattern by the actor Sanokawa Ichimatsu, who was at the height of his popularity during the Gembun and Kampō eras, 1736-1744; even now the pattern is called *ichimatsu* for his name.

The lower portion contains a fall scene including falcons, maples, and waterfalls, executed in resist-dye with occasional embroidery. The execution is superb; such details as the sharp eyes and beaks of the falcons and even the tassels attached to their legs are clearly brought out. The maples are both delicate and vivid. Nonetheless, the composition, as in the stylized presentation of the waterfalls, is more a matter of clothing design than a pictorial representation; the work does not approach the realm of picture-painting as closely as do pieces of a later age. (See catalogue 16, 38.)

Though the kimono is quite clearly divided into portions above and below the obi, a unifying final touch is added by the embroidery in gold and green yarns of "dandy's crests" or *date-mon* on the sleeves and center back. The word *date* in the sense of ostentatiousness or foppery is taken from the surname Date of the feudal lords of Sendai in northern Japan; Date Tsunamune was a notoriously flashy dresser of the Genroku period (1688-1704). The prefix *date* thereafter came to mean anything intended purely for decorative effect. *Date-mon* are decorative devices positioned similarly to or resembling family crests, but having no heraldic significance. In this instance the characters of the *date-mon* read, from right to left, "red falcon," "clever falcon," and "young falcon" *(kōyō, shunyō, jakuyō)* — phrases extolling and reflecting the virtues of the birds depicted in the lower portion.

10
**KOSODE with plum tree, water, and
    drying nets**
Imitation tie-dye *(suri-hitta)* **and
    embroidery**
White figured satin *(rinzu)*
Middle Edo   149.0 cm x 59.5 cm

Here the design is divided into upper and lower portions. In the upper portion is a blossoming plum tree on which are superimposed embroidered geometrical designs consisting of floral lozenges *(hanabishi)* in tortoise shell hexagons *(kikkō)*. In contrast, the lower portion displays a seashore motif, with drying nets and seashells tied together by strong, supple hand-inked lines suggesting swirling eddies.

In addition to embroidery with gold and colored yarns, the techniques used here include stenciled imitation tie-dye *(suri-hitta)*, a mechanical imitation of the time-consuming and costly finely knotted tie-dye *(hitta)* which had been banned by the sumptuary laws of 1683. While imitation tie-dye was clearly faster and less costly than real tie-dye, and was thus tolerated by the law, the effect is rather mechanical. The lines and spacing are too regular, and the center dot where the fabric would protrude through the tied knot is often missing or added later by hand. Moreover imitation tie-dye fails to reproduce the relief effect of real tie-dye so that the final result is flat.

Like the preceding piece, this kosode shows the increased influence of the obi in dividing the garment into clearly differentiated upper and lower halves. This was often accompanied, as in this example, by a marked contrast not only in design content but in mood or atmosphere of the two portions.

11
KOSODE with bridges over a stream,
  plum blossoms, and water plantains
Tie-dye *(hitta)* and embroidery
White silk crepe *(chirimen)*
Middle Edo   156.0 cm x 61.0 cm

The design here is based on the contrast between the straight lines of the criss-crossing planked bridges, the "Eight Bridges" or "*Yatsuhashi*" theme from the tenth century fiction *The Tales of Ise*, and the curves of the swirling water and graceful stems of water plantain (*omodaka; Sagittaria trifolia* L.; strictly arrowhead, a member of the water plantain family).

The planking of the bridges and leaves of the plantain are rendered in blue and red tie-dye *(hitta)*, while the water is stenciled in deep indigo blue. The pilings of the bridges are done in satin stitch embroidery; and the scattered sprays of plum blossoms and stems of the plantains are embroidered in gold and colored yarns. The embroidery adds variety of color and texture, though the design is achieved primarily through dyeing.

12
KOSODE with autumn maples
Resist-dye *(somenuki)* **and**
    embroidery
Green figured satin *(rinzu)*
Middle Edo   **147.0 cm x 62.0 cm**

The material is figured satin *(rinzu)* woven with a design of paulonia over a geometric hemp-leaf pattern *(asa-no-ha,* resembling a six-pointed star). The surface decoration consists of maples depicted in part by embroidery and in part by *somenuki* dyeing, in which a starch resist has been used to protect the portions to be left white, prior to the application of the green dye to the material.

Embroidered across the top in scarlet and gold are the first four characters of a verse by the great T'ang poet Po Chü-i (772-846), whom the Japanese of the Heian period (794-1185) held in highest esteem among the poets of China.

The forest seems tie-dyed in yellow,
    Cold, still clad with leaves;
The water lies a crystal blue,
    Clear, untouched by any breeze.[5]

Only the first line of the verse appears on the kosode. The second and third characters, read *kōkechi* in Japanese, comprise the classical term for tie dyeing. The poet's likening of nature's autumn coloration to the dyeing of silk make this a particularly appropriate literary allusion for a fall kimono.

13

KOSODE with bamboo among golden clouds
Attributed to Ogata Kōrin (1658-1716)

Hand painted with scattered gold
White figured satin (*rinzu*)
Middle Edo   166.0 cm x 63.0 cm

This kosode is notable in several respects. The ground is a white figured satin (*rinzu*) with an unusual woven motif of circular medallions with dragons among clouds. The design is of bamboo painted by hand in varying shades of India ink; the brushwork has been attributed to Ogata Kōrin, one of the leading and most individualistic artists of the Edo period. Finally flaked gold has been scattered here and there over the surface to create the effect of clouds in a technique reminiscent of that used by Kōrin in his painting of screens.

The work is unsigned and the attribution cannot be definitely established, but the design and expression clearly reflect the hand of a master. The brushwork is sure and accomplished conveying the impression of swift, unhesitating execution.

Kōrin was an inventive genius in a variety of mediums. Several anecdotes of his interest in kimono design are recorded, and a number of kosode more or less certainly attributed to his hand survive; notable is his multichrome rendition of autumn flowers on white figured silk (*aya*) preserved at the Tokyo National Museum. Other prominent artists whose textile designs or creations survive are Kōrin's leading follower Sakai Hōitsu (1761-1828) and the woodblock artist Andō Hiroshige (1797-1858).[6]

14
KATABIRA with sand bars and reeds
Resist-dye (*chaya-tsuji*) and
    embroidery
Light blue plain-woven ramie (*asa*)
Middle Edo   163.0 cm x 60.0 cm

The *katabira* is an unlined outer kimono for summer wear, usually made of fine bleached ramie. During the Edo period fabrics woven of ramie produced at Takashima near Lake Biwa and at Nara were especially noted for their quality.

The *chaya-tsuji* (or *chaya-zome*) dyeing technique, which had points of technical similarity with *yūzen* resist dyeing, was the proprietary technique of the wealthy Chaya merchant family, purveyors of clothing to the Imperial Palace in Kyoto; its secrets have been lost today. In the Edo period the wearing of clothing dyed in this method was severely restricted by the Tokugawa shoguns.

The present *katabira* is an excellent example of the application of the technique to the indigo dyeing of ramie. The white areas were all reserved with starch resist prior to immersion in the indigo dye bath.

Pines and cherries are scattered over sandy beaches in a spreading shore scene, containing also such vignettes of human activity as drying nets and salt pans. Ripples in the water's surface are executed with a delicacy suggesting silk crepe *(chirimen)*. The very limited use of embroidery here and there is also typical of the *chaya-tsuji* style, and adds a touch of color which softens the overall design. The sails scattered in the upper portion suggest the sea broadening into the distance.

15
KATABIRA with shore scene of
   boats, pine, and bamboo
Resist-dye *(chaya-tsuji)* and
   embroidery
White silk crepe *(chirimen)*
Middle Edo   156.0 cm x 62.0 cm

Though the effect is one of cool simplicity, this light summer kimono is in fact a product of the most painstaking and sophisticated craftsmanship; for all the undyed areas must first be covered with a protective starch resist before immersion of the whole in the indigo vat to produce the blue of the design.

For a design as detailed and delicate as this, it was not at all unusual for several months to be required for the application of the resist alone. The result is a truly extravagant garment for summer wear by a lady of the palace.

The extremely fine indigo-dyed lines of the present example are supremely exquisite, an effect enhanced by the sparing use of embroidery in gold and colored yarns.

16
KOSODE with "Eight Views of
Lake Biwa"
Resist-dye *(yūzen)*
White silk crepe *(chirimen)*
Middle Edo   **147.0 cm x 56.0 cm**

From the middle of the Edo period onward, resist-dye *(yūzen)* became one of the dominant techniques of kosode ornamentation. This is a representative masterwork of the genre in which all of the famous "Eight Views of Lake Biwa," "*Ōmi hakkei,*" are presented in detail on a single garment, done entirely in resist-dye except for embroidered floral embellishments and the purple tie-dyed clouds of the upper portion.

The famed and often stereotyped "Eight Views of Lake Biwa" consist of a series of eight scenic views from spots around the lute-shaped lake, across the mountains to the east of Kyoto in modern Shiga prefecture. The eight views concept originated in China with the "Eight Views of Hsiao-hsiang," a series of paintings of views in the Hsiao-hsiang area south of Lake Tung-t'ing in south central China by the Sung landscape painter Sung Ti. In the Japanese version the themes are the same but the places are different, having been transposed from Lake Tung-t'ing,

the largest lake in China, to Lake Biwa — the largest in Japan.

In this kosode the views of shore scenes around the lake are shown against the white ground in the upper part of the garment, interspersed with purple clouds; those related to the lake itself are shown against the blue waters of the skirt.

Thus in the outer or left front skirt[7] is depicted the "Evening Glow at Seta." Above this, in the center front of the kosode, is the "Night Rain at Karasaki"; while on the inner or right front skirt is found the "Bright and Breezy Day at Awazu." In the upper portion of the kosode, scattered among purple clouds suggesting mountain views, are the "Autumn Moon at Ishiyama," the "Evening Bell at Miidera," and in the distance, the "Evening Snows on Mount Hira." In the central portion of the back, filling the expanse between mountains and lake, are the "Geese Alighting at Katada," and on the rear skirt, the "Boats Returning to Yabase."

17
KOSODE with pines and bolts of silk
Tie-dye *(hitta)* **and embroidery**
White figured satin *(rinzu)*
Middle Edo   149.0 cm x 62.0 cm

The ornamentation of this kosode shows the beginnings of a recovery from the strict sumptuary regulations of 1683; there is a comparatively lavish use of finely knotted tie-dye and embroidery in couched gold.

The design is of partially unfurled bolts of silk among pine motifs. Both silk and pine are symbolically auspicious, and the com- bination is not infrequently encountered: it is also said to constitute a reference to the costumes of the Nō drama, with which the pine is closely associated.

The vivid reds of the upper and lower portions of this kosode contrast strikingly with the blue and black tones of the waist area.

18
KOSODE with pine and plum
Embroidery
Red figured satin (*rinzu*)
Late Edo   142.0 cm x 59.0 cm

The branches of the plum extend over the kimono as though entwined around the single pine. Though the plum blossoms foretell the eventual arrival of spring, the feeling is still wintry; the plum blossoms in February or early March.

The design is carried out in embroidery on figured satin woven with a pattern of flowers on key fretting; there is no use here of decorative dye techniques. The very simplicity of the embroidered ornamentation serves all the more to emphasize the subdued and spare colors of winter.

19
YOGI with nandina sprays
Resist dye *(somenuki)* and
    embroidery
Green silk crepe *(chirimen)*
Late Edo   142.0 cm x 60.0 cm

The *yogi* is a padded kimono intended to be thrown over the bedding on wintry nights: a coverlet, not an article of apparel. The sleeves are fully sewn to the body, rather than left open in the back as in furisode and many kosode. The arms are not normally put through the sleeves. In this example the white silk lining is extended at the cuffs and hem to provide broad white borders.

The design, executed in resist-dye and embroidery, is of numerous sprays of nandina *(nan-ten; Nandina domestica)*. The vivid red berries of the nandina cling tenaciously to the branches throughout the snowy winter; and accordingly the shrub is regarded as a symbol of wifely devotion and fidelity and is often adopted as a design motif for articles intended for women.

Yet it is not only as a shrub symbolizing fidelity that the nandina is a particularly appropriate motif for winter bedding. The Japanese name *nan-ten* (literally "south skies") may, through a play on the sound of the words, be taken to imply "the aversion of troubles" *(nan wo tenzuru)*, suggesting an ability of the shrub to ward off nightmares by changing them into happy dreams. In this sense, too, the nandina is a felicitous theme for a coverlet.

20
FURISODE with bamboo shades
among pine, bamboo, and plum
Tie-dye *(hitome-shibori)* **and**
embroidery
Scarlet figured satin *(rinzu)*
Late Edo   159.0 cm x 62.5 cm

The ground here is a typical figured satin woven with a key-fret pattern *(saya-gata)*.

The basic design element consists of the bamboo shades or screens used as partitions between palace apartments, depicted in one-eye tie-dye *(hitome-shibori)*. To these have been added the familiar and auspicious combination of pine, bamboo, and plum *(shōchikubai)*, executed in tie-dye and embroidery of gold and colored yarns. Finally, clouds of gold dust have been scattered here and there adding a further artistic touch.

This furisode is typical of the designs favored by ladies of the Late Edo, incorporating felicitous symbols with a touch of nostalgia.

21
KOSODE with plovers amidst
   water reeds
Embroidery
Yellow silk figured gauze *(sha)*
Late Edo   157.0 cm x 60.0 cm

The material is a very light figured gauze woven with a fine pattern of plum, cherry blossoms, and pine needles. The embroidered design is of water weeds *(kuromo; Hydrilla verticillata)* with plovers and gives a feeling of cool neatness conducive to comfort and composure in Japan's intensely humid, hot summers.

The very brevity and simplicity of the embroidery infuses the work with refinement. The crisp design and light colors combine successfully with the sheer fabric of this summer kimono.

22
CHILD'S FESTIVE KIMONO with
tortoise medallions
Embroidery
Crimson figured satin (*rinzu*)
Late Edo   96.0 cm x 51.0 cm

A furisode-style garment for a child to wear when visiting shrines or strolling abroad on occasions such as the New Year or the Seven-five-three *(Shichi-go-san)* festival, a special gala day for children of three, five, and seven.

On the latter occasion, celebrated now on November 15th, important transition points were marked in the life of a child. On this day in their third year children of both sexes were considered to pass from babyhood to childhood, and the style of hairdressing was accordingly changed. Boys in their fifth year first donned the lower part of adult dress (*hakama*, corresponding to western trousers); and girls in their fifth year were first dressed in an adult-style kimono with an obi.[8] Was this perhaps the purpose for which the present kimono was made? The size is about right for a girl of seven.

The ground is a figured satin with key fretting and stylized flowers. The surface design is entirely embroidered and consists of stylized sea tortoises, symbols of good luck and long life, worked into large circular medallions scattered over the kimono.

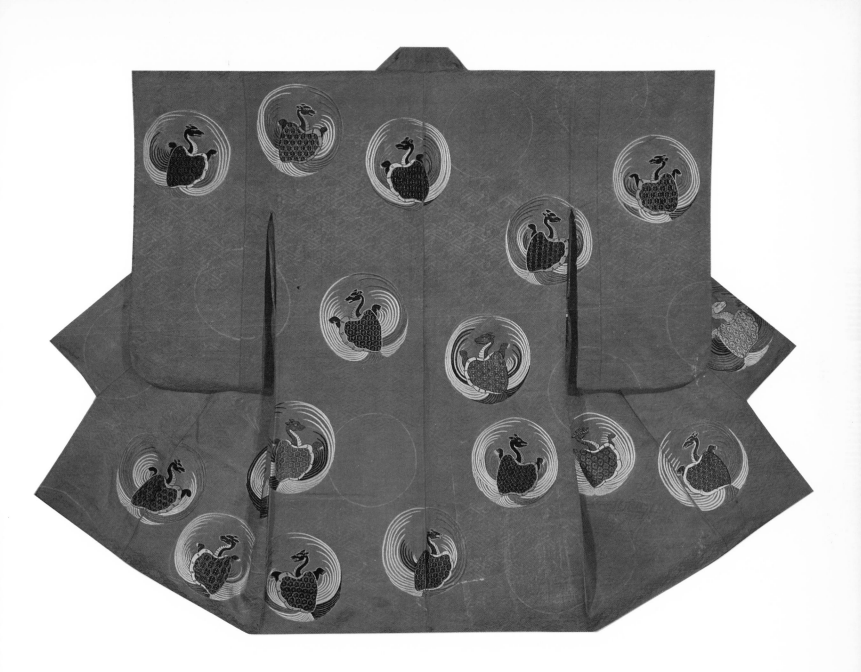

23
CHILD'S FESTIVE KIMONO with
  floral medallions
Resist-dye *(yūzen)*
Crimson silk crepe *(chirimen)*
Late Edo   77.0 cm x 55.0 cm

The color of the ground is a brilliant and festive red; but the circular medallions of paulonia, plum, chrysanthemum, and camellia, executed in resist-dye, are rather on the small side. Normally for a child's festive garment the medallion designs would be larger, and the design should incorporate auspicious elements, just as in the preceding piece, catalogue 22.

Moreover, the sleeves are almost long enough for an adult, while the body is roughly half adult length, and the design appears cut off at the hem.

Clearly this garment has been recycled: a phenomenon not unknown in the West, where an adult dress is made over as a splendid festive costume for a small child. A happy ending for this design.

24
**CHILD'S KATABIRA with drying
   nets and plovers**
Particolor and resist dye *(somenuki)*
Plain weave *(asa)*
Late Edo   86.0 cm x 36.5 cm*

The dyed design, a seaside scene with plovers among drying nets, is appropriate for summer. The zig-zag lines separating the black upper portion from the crimson ground of the lower body and sleeves lend a sharp, masculine note suggesting that this is a boy's kimono. For a kimono this size a single width of fabric suffices, and there is no center seam in the back.

The typical decorative technique used for *katabira* (summer kimono, usually of ramie) is the *chaya-tsuji* resist-dye method based on indigo (catalogue 14, 15); but the division here into contrasting black and crimson grounds is reminiscent of the particolor dye *(somewake)* of the Momoyama and Early Edo periods (catalogue 2). The cut and the resist-reserved crests on the back, however, together with the confinement of the design to the lower portion, show this to be a Late Edo piece. It is an elegantly designed and finely crafted robe for a boy of five or six.

*Since there is no center seam in the back of this kimono, the sleeve length shown is half the width from cuff to cuff.

25
KOSODE with pine sprays
Overall tie-dye (*sō-hitta*)
Purple figured satin (*rinzu*)
Late Edo   149.0 cm x 60.0 cm

This and the following three kimono have been made using the technique known as *sō-hitta* (overall finely knotted tie-dye) or *sō-kanoko* (overall fawn spot). In this exceedingly difficult and time-consuming technique the entire surface of the material between the lines of the design is painstakingly gathered into hundreds of thousands of fine, regular knots, tightly bound one by one with several wrappings of thread to prevent the dye from penetrating. Merely the preparation of such a piece for dyeing commonly required more than a year.

It should be understood that once such a piece was initiated the same artisan must continue the work without interruption; a change of workers — or even a brief illness — could result in an irreparable alteration of the rhythm of the tying and the evenness of the results. After the garment had been dipped in the dye bath to color the unprotected portions, the cutting of the tying threads without harming the material was an equally exacting task.

The repeated stylized pine spray motif of this kosode has been carried out with impressive exactitude; the very repetitiveness of the design reduces the allowances for error in tying, yet the work has been done with such accuracy that the outlines of the design have the fineness of line drawings.

26
KOSODE with shells, seaweed,
 and bamboo
Overall tie-dye *(sō-hitta)*
Purple plain-weave silk
Late Edo   144.0 cm x 61.0 cm

This kimono has been put together from pieces of material bearing two different designs, perhaps originally intended for two kimono. The body bears a design of shells and seaweed, while the sleeves and neckband *(eri)* have a bamboo motif.

The extremely laborious and therefore costly tie-dye technique used here was rigidly banned by the strict sumptuary laws of the third year of Tenna, 1683, and it was the need for an alternative to elaborate tie-dye and embroidery which provided much of the impetus for the development of *yūzen* resist-dye.

Though the strictness of the sumptuary regulations and the severity of their enforce-ment varied, the use of finely knotted tie-dyeing *(hitta)* was confined throughout the Middle Edo to comparatively minor portions of the design, and various painting and stenciling techniques were developed to pro-duce an imitation *hitta* at lowered cost. Such elaborate works as the present piece could be carried out only in secret.

By the beginning of the nineteenth century, however, the regulations were widely flouted or forgotten and exquisite and extravagant works such as the present group of four were again produced.

27
KOSODE with pine, bamboo, plum,
   and cranes
Overall tie-dye *(sō-hitta)*
Crimson figured satin *(rinzu)*
Late Edo   **160.0 cm x 60.0 cm**

In this exquisite example of overall tie-dye cranes, symbolic of longevity, are depicted flying among the felicitous combination of pine, bamboo, and plum *(shōchikubai)*.

An immense degree of skill must have been required to produce the fluent and harmonious pattern of this kosode. Bearing in mind those portions to be left untied to form the lines of the design, the artisan toiled patiently and almost endlessly to tie each of the hundreds of thousands of individual knots where the material was to be protected from the dye. The evenness of the lines of the design is a manifestation of the control and careful craftsmanship applied in carrying out the design.

When tying was complete the entire work was dipped into the dye, then dried. After this, each knot was individually snipped and released. Even though a single color is used, the result is a splendid, even extraordinary, costume.

28
FURISODE with a single pine
Overall tie-dye *(sō-hitta)*
Purple figured satin *(rinzu)*
Late Edo   149.5 cm x 61.0 cm

In this final example of overall finely knotted tie-dye the subtle flavor of this hand technique, impossible to achieve mechanically, can be well appreciated.

As an accommodation to the Tenna sumptuary regulations of 1683 a number of imitation tie-dye techniques had been developed, in which dye was applied by hand painting or stencil. Yet while a fair imitation of the *hitta* pattern was thus achieved, the surface of the material remained flat and the effect was somewhat weak, without texture.

In true *hitta* tie-dye — as in this example — the surface effect of the process is virtually permanent. The tightly tied knotting thread actually shrinks during the dyeing process, further constricting the material and producing a shimmering relief. The fine diagonal rows of knots in this furisode provide a delicate and fully satisfying illustration of this point. The occasional irregular spots, where the dye has penetrated or the knot perhaps came untied, do not detract from the design but rather serve to emphasize the unrelenting demand of the technique and the uniqueness of the results.

29
**FURISODE with stream and bush
    clover**
Tie-dye *(hitome-shibori)*, **resist-dye
    (yūzen), and embroidery**
White figured satin *(rinzu)*
Late Edo   157.0 cm x 65.0 cm

The material is figured satin woven with a larger than usual pattern of stylized flowers over the typical diagonal key fretting *(saya-gata)*. The bold design of the broadly meandering stream is reminiscent of the style of Early Edo kimono, but the bush clover *(hagi; Lespedeza nipponica)* which fills the intervals between turns of the stream is executed in *yūzen* resist dye with a delicacy which subtly contrasts with the florid windings of the stream and clearly identifies this as a Late Edo work.

The stream has been executed in tie-dye with indigo; a ripple effect is produced by rows of fine ties *(hitome-shibori)*. A further decorative effect is achieved through the occasional use of embroidery with gold thread for some of the leaves of the bush clover. The very fine stems of the clover have been drawn in by hand.

The unity and sweep of the whole conception are remarkable, and it is difficult to imagine what sort of obi could be selected to complement rather than detract from this design. Moreover the tucks normally taken in the body of the kimono under the sash would raise the skirt, affecting the continuity of pattern between body and sleeves. It is, therefore, believed that this robe, while technically a furisode in cut and construction, was worn on ceremonial occasions as an over-kimono or cloak, *uchikake*, held together by the hands; see also catalogue 30.

30
FURISODE with cresting stream
and iris
Tie-dye *(hitome-shibori)*, resist-dye
(yūzen), and embroidery
White figured satin *(rinzu)*
Late Edo   170.0 cm x 62.0 cm

This design, on a ground of figured satin woven with key-fret and floral designs, is superficially similar to that of the preceding furisode, catalogue 29; but here the stream is a vivid red, and occupies a far larger portion of the surface. The rush of the stream is suggested both by the startling color and by the rows of fine white ties.

In contrast to the semi-stylized presentation of the water, the irises *(kakitsubata; Iris laevigata)* which line the banks and fill the remainder of the design are depicted in realistic and charming detail. The purple flowers are embroidered, while the leaves and stems are done in hand-painted *yūzen* resist dyeing — the outlines having first been marked off with fine lines of resist paste after which the subtly varied light green dyes were applied by hand.

The iris and the urgency of the red water suggest a scene toward the end of the Japanese rainy season in early June. The stream, swollen almost to overflowing by a just-ended downpour, rushes down the back of the garment in a torrent which calls to mind the sodden and overcast rainy season. The gentle iris, however, blooming beside the water, provide relief from the rather oppressive seasonal feeling, and add a touch of elegant composure most welcome in the summer.

As with the preceding, catalogue 29, it is difficult to imagine an obi which would enhance rather than detract from this design. This furisode too was most probably worn in the manner of an over-kimono *(uchikake)*, allowed to trail somewhat behind the wearer in a manner which would display the swirling water to stunning effect.

It should be noted, however, that while both this and the preceding item are thought to have been worn unsashed as outer robes, they are both furisode in cut and construction; both lack the heavy wadded lining of the hem characteristic of the more formal and elaborate garments technically known as *uchikake.*

31
KOSHIMAKI with myriad treasures
Embroidery
Red-tinged black plain weave silk
Late Edo   157.0 cm x 62.0 cm

The *koshimaki* (waist wrap) is a style of kimono which evolved from the outer robe *(uchikake)* worn on full-dress occasions over the ordinary kimono and obi (catalogue 29 and 30). When worn as an *uchikake* such an outer robe was draped from the shoulders and held together by the hands, without a sash. In the *koshimaki* style it was allowed to slip from the shoulders entirely, being held in place by a sash so that it enveloped only the lower half of the body, in a cooler style suitable for summer.

Koshimaki in the richly embellished style of this and the following example, catalogue 32, were worn by ladies of the palace over unlined summer kimono *(katabira)*, normally of ramie dyed by the *chaya-tsuji* resist method (catalogue 14, 15).

The typically dark ground is completely covered with the various elements of the "myriad treasures" *(takarazukushi)*, richly embroidered in gold and colored yarns. Included among these treasures, which have magical or auspicious associations, are: the hat and cloak of invisibility *(kakure-gasa* and *kakure-mino)*, which render the wearer invisible; the hammer of fortune *(uchide-no-kozuchi)*, which pours forth riches with every shake; the magic or flaming pearl *(hōju)* of Buddhism; keys; silks; cloves and other South Seas exotica; and the "seven jewels" *(shippō:* gold, silver, lapis lazuli, crystal, coral, agate, and pearl, in one of several listings), here stylized into purely geometric designs.

32
KOSHIMAKI with myriad treasures
    and crests
Embroidery
Red-tinged black plain weave silk
Late Edo   165.0 cm x 63.5 cm

Like the preceding example, catalogue 31, this *koshimaki* was made for summer court use, to be worn together with a ramie *katabira*. Toward the end of the Edo period this combination became increasingly formalized and evolved eventually into a summer uniform for palace attendants.

As this formalization proceeded a new and unique style for the wearing of the *koshimaki* developed. The obi which bound the *katabira* was knotted firmly at the small of the back, and straw-reinforced paper tubes were inserted into the ends of the sash so that they stood out stiffly to left and right behind the wearer. The sleeves of the *koshimaki* were arranged over these wing-like projections, which extended some distance to both

sides, and the body of the *koshimaki* was secured to the obi by a cord attached to the neck-piece *(eri)*. Thus what had originally been an over-kimono worn wrapped around the waist became no more than an ornamental train.

This example like the preceding, catalogue 31, is typical of the conventionalized *koshimaki*. The plain weave silk ground has been dyed a deep black and entirely covered by rich embroidery in the myriad treasures theme. Here the usual elements of the theme are augmented by scattered family crests bearing the familiar triple wild ginger *(aoi)* leaves of the Tokugawa shoguns, as well as the stylized swallow-tail butterfly.

33
**KOSODE with cherry blossom, pine,
 and iris**
Resist-dye *(somenuki)*, **imitation tie-
 dye** *(suri-hitta)*, **and embroidery**
**Light yellow-green silk crepe
 *(chirimen)***
Late Edo   145.0 cm x 59.0 cm

Here the design has first been sketched in with starch resist prior to dyeing the yellow-green ground color. The nuance possible with this resist technique *(somenuki)* is evident in the delicacy of the pine sprays and the evenness of the swirling lines indicating the water.

The design is of a stream in late spring or early summer. A pavillion stands beside the stream in the lower right of the design, implying the presence of man in this vernal scene.

The design is stylized, but in the very stylization may be seen the practiced hand of the skilled craftsman.

34
**KATABIRA with scene of
   Mount Hōrai**
**Resist-dye, imitation tie-dye (*suri-
   hitta*), and embroidery**
White plain-weave ramie (*asa*)
Late Edo   157.0 cm x 61.5 cm

The design of this kimono, executed in embroidery and a variety of dyeing techniques including resist-dye and stenciled imitation tie-dye, includes a familiar combination of symbols of fortune and long life. To the pine, bamboo, and plum *(shōchikubai)*, symbolizing respectively long life and constancy, rectitude, and harmony, are added cranes and sea tortoises, said to live for one thousand and ten thousand years. The waves splashing upon rocky shores along the hem suggest an island, from which we may conclude that the design is an evocation of Mount Hōrai (Chinese P'eng-lai), the mythic island paradise in the far reaches of the Yellow Sea between China and the Korean peninsula.

From the motif and the use of summery ramie, it may be assumed that this *katabira* was created for an elegant summer wedding.

35
**KATABIRA with sylvan landscape
   on an autumnal evening
Resist-dye, stenciled imitation tie-dye
   (*suri-hitta*), and embroidery
White plain weave ramie (*asa*)
Late Edo   172.0 cm x 63.5 cm**

This is a summer kimono of bleached ramie decorated with indigo resist-dye, embroidery in gold and colored yarns, and restricted use of stenciled imitation tie-dye.

The design would seem intended to induce relief from the humid heat of summer, and suggests the pictorial realization of a plaintive tune from long ago; a tune played upon the *koto*, the long zither of Japan, while admiring the autumn moon in a sylvan hermitage far from the capital.

36
FURISODE with seasonal landscape
Resist-dye *(somenuki)*, imitation tie-
dye *(suri-hitta)*, and embroidery
Green silk gauze *(ro)*
Late Edo   176.5 cm x 62.0 cm

The material is *ro* silk gauze, a soft material in which the warp yarns are periodically crossed, dyed green with a greyish tinge. The design is achieved in part by resist reservation of white lines *(somenuki)*, together with a limited use of imitation tie-dye, and lavish embroidery filling the entire surface with a rich abundance of detail.

Nonetheless, despite this richness, there is a feeling of melancholy in coloration and design, which suggests that this is a summer garment for a woman past her fullest years.

This is an example of the dyed and embroidered landscape design known as *Gosho-toki*, "Views of the Imperial Palace," a rich but calm and often nostalgic style of Late Edo.

37
FURISODE with fishnets drying
   on the shore and swallows
Resist-dye *(somenuki)* and
   embroidery
Purple figured silk gauze *(ro)*
Late Edo   172.0 cm x 62.0 cm

This is a light summer kimono of figured silk gauze woven with a pattern of butterflies on wistaria lattice *(fuji-tasuki)*.

The design, accomplished with very limited use of resist-dye and detailed embroidery, is of a shore scene appropriate for summer. It has been executed in the formal "high skirt" *(taka-suso)* style, and covers the skirt of the garment but does not extend into the upper portion. This is a reflection both of the restrictive effects of tightening sumptuary regulations and of the increasing influence of the widening obi on costume design, a development which was eventually to draw the primary attention away from the kosode itself.

In the late Edo period the use of resist-reserved family crests *(mon)*—in the back center and sleeves and often on both breasts in the front—became a regular feature. Here the triple wild ginger *(aoi)* leaves indicate that this was a robe of a high-born young lady related to the Tokugawa shoguns. The use of purple for the ground color is also indicative of high rank.

The variegated yellow-greens of the pines and the gold of the thatched boat awning serve to soften the design, while the white throats of the swallows provide contrasting accents. This is an elegant and restrained summer robe of the early nineteenth century, without a touch of the flashiness which colored more common works of this period.

38
KOSODE with views of Yoshiwara
Resist-dye *(yūzen)* and embroidery
Brown silk crepe *(chirimen)*
Late Edo   160.0 cm x 61.0 cm

The design, on brown silk crepe, is of urban vignettes, showing the earthen embankment and main gate of the Yoshiwara pleasure quarter of Edo (Tokyo) from a bird's eye perspective. It is a work of exceedingly detailed craftsmanship. The primary technique employed is resist-dye *(yūzen)*, in which are depicted the scenery, the houses, and the shops, including even such fine details as the decorative curtains *(noren)* swaying gently before the sliding shop doors. Some of the trees, the people, and minute indoor details such as a smoking tray complete with bamboo-stemmed pipe are rendered in embroidery.

This is a masterwork; even the facial expressions and finger movements of the denizens of the quarter are clearly depicted in the embroidery. This kimono—perhaps the most often illustrated of the Kanebo treasures —appears to have been created to bring pleasure as much from the viewing as from the wearing of it.

39
**FURISODE with a border design of
    butterflies on red**
**Resist-dye *(yūzen)*, imitation tie-dye
    (suri-hitta), and embroidery**
White figured satin *(rinzu)*
Late Edo   152.0 cm x 59.0 cm

The material is a supple white figured satin woven with a pattern of interlocked circles *(wa-chigai)*. Brilliant red decorative areas have been added by dyeing within cloud-shaped borders at the edges of the garment. These areas are further embellished with designs of butterflies and scrolling vines *(karakusa)* done in resist-dye *(yūzen)*, imitation tie-dye *(suri-hitta)*, and embroidery with gold yarns.

The kimono is unlined, except in the areas of the decoration; here lining has been specially attached, with precise replication of the outer ornamentation. It is notable that the positioning of the butterflies is identical on both surface and lining. This elaborate decorative technique was particularly effective as the wearer strolled along, holding up the hem of the garment to reveal the lining.

40
**KOSODE with hem design of stream
    and flowering plants**
Resist-dye (*somenuki*) **and
    embroidery**
Purple plain-weave silk
Late Edo   161.0 cm x 62.5 cm

With the gradual widening of the obi the focus of attention in costume design eventually shifted away from the kosode to the obi itself. The combination of changing fashion and strict, often capricious, sumptuary regulations led to the evolution of kimono in darker colors with decoration confined to the hem. Such designs balanced nicely with the elaborate coiffure of the wearer and avoided competition with the obi.

This evolution began in the eighteenth century (catalogue 9, 10) and reached its peak in the first half of the nineteenth. By the end of the Edo period the outer garments of even the most privileged classes, other than those for ceremonial occasions, conformed to this style. This and the following three pieces are typical: muted, even somber colors, with resist-reserved family crests and with other decoration only at the borders of the skirt. In the context of a sober and restrained public style of life, gaiety and splendor were reserved for private enjoyment.

In this example the material is plain-woven silk dyed a rich purple, with a hem design created by resist-dye reservation of white areas and embroidery with gold and colored yarns. The design features running water and herbal motifs of orchid, bamboo, chrysanthemum, and plum—symbolic of spring, summer, fall, and winter respectively.

41
**KOSODE with border design of
  shore scenes**
Embroidery
Aubergine figured satin (*rinzu*)
Late Edo   150.5 cm x 60.0 cm

The border design of shore scenes including rocks, boats, temples, and trees has
been carried out by embroidery in an understated style which resembles line drawing.
The material itself is figured satin *(rinzu)*
with an overall woven pattern of key fretting
(saya-gata), on which are superimposed oval
medallions of wild ginger *(aoi)* leaves and
butterflies. This is a traditional Japanese motif
reminiscent of late Heian (twelfth century).

The family crests in the upper portion
indicate that this is an outer garment; with a
liberally padded hem, it was meant to trail
along the floor. It is conjectured that this
kosode was worn by a palace maid-servant.

42
KOSODE with elaborated crests
Embroidery
Dark green silk damask *(donsu)*
Late Edo   157.5 cm x 65.0 cm

Donsu is a damask-type weave using warp and weft yarns of contrasting colors, producing a variegated or changeable color effect. The use of *donsu* in outer garments began in the eighteenth century.

The woven design of the material in this kosode is a typically fine *donsu* pattern in the cypress fence *(higaki)* motif, incorporating gold yarns placed at widely spaced intervals.

It is a lustrous material conveying a high sense of dignity.

The crests in the upper portion are composed of crane medallions in gold combined with pearls in a personal design created to resemble a family crest. This is believed to have been the kimono of an older woman with many years of service in the palace.

43
KOSODE with border design of floral rondels
Tie-dye *(shibori-zome)*, resist-dye *(somenuki)*, and embroidery
Purple and light blue silk crepe *(chirimen)* with warp stripes of uncultivated tussah
Late Edo   146.0 cm x 60.5 cm

The vertical stripes in the crepe material have been created by use of "wild silk" (tussah) yarns in the warp. Tussah, produced by a species of moth not directly related to the domesticated silkworm, does not take dye as readily as does true silk.[9]

The body and sleeves are a brownish purple color adorned only by the vertical light stripes and reserved family crests in the usual positions; the skirt has a wide border of light blue with embroidered floral rondels and broken lattice motifs *(yabure wa-chigai)*.

Both the purple and blue ground colors have been applied by tie-dye; but this is not the precise, drawn-stitch tie-dye used to create the carefully delineated grounds of the parti-color styles of Early Edo (catalogue 1 and 2). Here instead, the fabric has been loosely gathered and tied, allowing the dyes to bleed into the white zone separating the two principal color areas.

The striped ground of this kosode would serve all the better to enhance the splendor of a wide and decorative obi.

NOTES

Translator's note:

The descriptions of the individual items in this catalogue are based on the observations of Professor Nishimura, who is superbly qualified as commentator both by his expertise in the field and by his deep personal familiarity with the Kanebo Collection.

In translating and adapting Professor Nishimura's remarks for an American audience I have attempted both to satisfy the curiosity and to whet the further interest of the reader through addition of supplementary information which is part of the Japanese cultural fabric but less familiar abroad. It is perhaps inevitable that I have thereby introduced distortions and misperceptions, for which Professor Nishimura has my apologies. I would ask the reader to allot credit for all insights to him; and to assign blame for all errors to me.

I should like also to acknowledge indebtedness to Miss Kajitani Nobuko of the Textile Conservation Department, The Metropolitan Museum of Art, and to Mr. Frank Yorichika of the East Asian Library, Columbia University; they too bear no responsibility for any shortcomings, and this catalogue could only have benefited by fuller acceptance of the assistance they so willingly proffered.

The notes which follow are intended to suggest avenues for further inquiry. Detailed citations of Japanese and Chinese sources have been omitted in the belief that these are unnecessary to those prepared to use them, and unneeded by others.

(JSH)

1. See Japan Textile Color Design Center, *Textile Designs of Japan* (for full particulars of this and other works cited in shortened form in these Notes, see Bibliography), 1:34-35. The monumental *Textile Designs of Japan*, in three superbly illustrated volumes, sets the standard of scholarly excellence to which later Western workers in this field must aspire.

2. See Kyoto kokuritsu hakubutsukan, comp., *Kyō no senshoku-bi*, p. 185, commentary on no. 36 (in Japanese).

3. The *Wakan rōeishū (Collection of Chinese and Japanese Poems for Recitation)* was compiled by the prominent Heian poet Fujiwara no Kintō (966-1041), most probably in 1018 or shortly thereafter (though traditional sources assign the date of 1013). An anthology of 216 Japanese *waka* and 588 passages of Chinese poetry and prose — 234 by Chinese authors and 354 by Japanese — it consists of two books further divided into sections devoted to each of the four seasons and to a variety of miscellaneous topics.

The recitation of poetry at social gatherings was a popular aristocratic pastime in the Heian period, and the arrangement of the work was intended to facilitate selection of passages appropriate to the particular season or occasion. The poem cited here, a pair of couplets in Chinese style by the Heian poet Minamoto no Fusaakira, actually forms two consecutive selections in the *Wakan rōeishū*—each couplet of two seven-character lines being presented as an independent entry — and is found under "Flowers" *(hana)* in the "Spring" section of the first book.

Embroidered on the kosode, catalogue 7, are the first three characters of the second couplet.

The poem, evoking a connection between the weaver's skill and the quintessentially Japanese image of falling cherry blossoms, is one of obvious appeal to practitioners of the textile arts.

4. The poem, by Yoshishige no Yasutane (d. 997) is found under "Congratulations" *(iwai)* in the "Miscellany" section of the second book of the *Wakan rōeishū* (see preceding note). The Chōseiden (Chinese Ch'ang-sheng-tien) was erected in 742 at the Huang-ching Palace near the T'ang capital of Ch'ang-an. The original Gate of Lasting Youth (Furōmon, Chinese Pu-lao men) was one of the gates of the T'ang "Eastern Capital" of Lo-yang; the name was subsequently adopted for a gate within the Heian palace of ancient Kyoto.

Some older editions of the *Wakan rōeishū* have a variant reading at the end of the first line which gives "spring and autumn linger"; the translation in Mizoguchi, *Design Motifs*, p. 78, is based on such a variant. There is little doubt, however, that "springs and autumns abound" is the original and correct reading. The phrase is well attested in Chinese historical literature, and can be traced to the *Historical Record (Shih chi)* of Ssu-ma Ch'ien (ca. 145-90 B.C.), where it is used to explain the unpreparedness of a youthful emperor to rule the world. The variant appears to have arisen from the visual similarity of the characters *ryū* ("linger") and *tomu* ("abound"), and from the attractive parallel in meaning between "linger" and "slow down."

For the relationship between *aoi* and the Tokugawa, see Glossary under "*aoi*."

An intriguing alternative interpretation of the design of the kosode, catalogue 8, has been proposed by Miss Jean Mailey. The term *aoi* includes a number of botanically unrelated species, and the representation here is not sufficiently specific to preclude reference to the aquatic *mizu-aoi*, a relative of the water hyacinth. This and the flowing panelling of the background, together with the zig-zag motif and the classical poem alluding to the emperor, may well suggest the Heian pastime of floating poems back and forth across a lazy stream. The possibility of such an alternative interpretation, which can only coexist happily with that of the catalogue citation, merely adds to the charm and appeal of this kosode.

5. See *Wakan rōeishū*, under "Autumn leaves" *(kōyō)* in the "Fall" section of the first book. Po Chü-i is by far the best-represented Chinese poet in the *Wakan rōeishū*; 135 of the 234 passages by Chinese authors are his.

The verse quoted is actually the third couplet — that is, the fifth and sixth seven-character lines — of a sixteen-line poem written by Po "while floating on the Great Lake" and addressed to his great friend Yüan Chen (779-831), referred to by his literary style Wei-chih *(Fan T'ai-hu shu-shih chi Wei-chih)*. The poem was written during a brief interlude late in 825 (or possibly early 826; the feeling is as much of winter as of fall) when the poet was able to take some

time after a grueling year as Governor of Soochow to go boating on the Great Lake (T'ai-hu) west of the city. The experience was a pleasant one, in fine wintry weather: "I'll tell you one thing," he writes to Yüan Chen, "that you will envy: I have spent five nights on these clear waves, under the bright moon." For the context, see Arthur Waley, *The Life and Times of Po Chü-i, 772-846 A.D.* (London: George Allen and Unwin, 1949), p. 164.

The immediate source for the inscription on this kosode, catalogue 12, is not the poem itself but the excerpt in the *Wakan rōeishū*. Curiously, both on the kosode and in the *rōeishū* the Japanese version is written slightly differently from the Chinese. The second character (on the right shoulder) is a purely Japanese character, unknown in China. An elaboration of the character for *shibori* ("tie-dye"), it is the first character of *kōkechi*, the classical Japanese term for tie-dyeing. In the Chinese texts, however (see *e.g.*, the *Ssu-pu ts'ung-k'an* edition of Po's works, in which the poem appears in *chüan* 54, folio 16), the character used is *chia*, "squeeze," which in Japanese is the first character of *Kyōkechi* ("squeeze resist"; see Glossary), a resist technique using carved boards which was known in the eighth century in both countries.

This suggests that *kyōkechi* and *kōkechi* may originally have meant the same thing, "squeeze resist," *kōkechi* being a specifically Japanese variant emphasizing tying rather than squeezing and subsequently expanded in meaning to include a number of related techniques; indeed, the modern Japanese equivalent of *kyōkechi, itajime-shibori,* is regarded as a sub-category of tie-dyeing, *shibori-zome.*

6. For anecdotes of Kōrin and his involvement with costume design see, *e.g.,* Helen Benton Minnich, *Japanese Costume,* pp. 274 and 280-281. Mrs. Minnich's admirable study, the product of a long and close association with the pioneer scholar and collector of kimono Nomura Shōjirō, remains unsurpassed in breadth, wealth of illustration and anecdote, and grace of authorship. It is unquestionably the standard Western-language introduction to the study of Japanese costume.

For the Kōrin Kosode of the Tokyo National Museum see Minnich, pp. 273-274 and fig. 111. This kosode has been published often; see, *e.g.,* Japan Textile Color Design Center, *Textile Designs of Japan,* vol. 1, plate 4.2; or Tokyo kokuritsu hakubutsukan, *Nihon no senshoku* (1974), plate 48.

Signed kimono by Sakai Hōitsu (hand painting on white satin) and Andō Hiroshige (embroidered cotton under-kimono, design by Hiroshige) were included in the Nomura collection: see Minnich, pp. 274 and 317 and figs. 112, 119, and 120. For the Hōitsu kosode see also the just-cited *Nihon no senshoku,* plate 49.

7. Both men's and women's kimono are worn with the left side overlapping the right, in the Western "man's" fashion; the style is reversed only in the dressing of corpses. Few feminine foreign residents of Japan will have avoided the experience, after having unconsciously donned Japanese dress in the Western "woman's" right-over-left style, of being urgently detained and summarily undressed and rearranged by a kindly but horrified grandmother, aghast at the visitor's having dressed herself as though deceased.

8. See, for instance, Charles J. Dunn, *Everyday Life in Traditional Japan,* p. 166.

9. True silk is produced by the species *Bombyx mori,* which feeds on the leaves of the mulberry. Japanese tussah is taken from the cocoons of the oak-leaf eating *Antheraea yamamai.*

GLOSSARY

Aoi:

The name applied to a number of generally unrelated botanical species having more or less heart-shaped leaves, including the hollyhock *(tachi-aoi; Althaea rosea)*; a member of the aquatic pickerel-weed family *(mizu-aoi; Monochoria korsakowii* Regel et Maack)*; and the two-leaved wild ginger *(futaba-aoi; Asarum caulescens)*.

While both dictionaries and modern Japanese usage identify *aoi* most closely with the hollyhock, this identification is inappropriate for the Edo and earlier periods. In connection both with the annual *aoi-matsuri* May festival of Kyoto, which dates from Heian times, and with the three-leaved *mitsuba-aoi* crest of the Tokugawa, the plant in question is clearly the two-leaved wild ginger, which is native to the mountains around Kyoto and throughout much of Japan.

The association of the *aoi*, wild ginger, with the Tokugawa family of the Edo shoguns is supposed to date from the time of Hidetada, father of the first shogun Ieyasu. Legend relates that upon his return from a victorious battle he was served a meal of cakes from a tray decorated with three wild ginger leaves. Struck by the pattern of leaves upon the tray, and associating it with his victory, he adopted the design for his crest *(mon)*. It remains the family crest today.

For the *aoi* in association with the Tokugawa house see catalogue 8, 32, and 37; for its incorporation in a motif reminiscent of Heian times, see catalogue 41.

Asa:

In the narrowest sense, hemp; and in the broadest, all of the bast fibers — fibers obtained from the phloem or inner bark of certain plants, including hemp, jute, flax, and ramie.

Among the bast fibers two were of major economic significance in pre-modern Japan. These were hemp *(taima; Cannabis sativa* L.)* and ramie *(karamushi* or *choma; Boehmeria nivea;* sometimes called China grass in English).

Until the introduction of cotton the clothing of the ordinary Japanese people was made primarily from *asa* — meaning in this case primarily hemp, which was comparatively easily worked and produced a coarse, strong, brownish material — but including also ramie for better quality materials as well as several other fibers. During the sixteenth century cotton began to be imported in significant quantity from China and Korea, and thereafter gradually displaced hemp and the other bast fibers from ordinary clothing. With the development of a technically more sophisticated textile industry and the spread of cotton, the application of bast fibers gradually shifted from coarses fabrics for work clothing to ever finer materials, and hemp yielded its place to ramie — a stronger fiber, more difficult to process, but readily bleached to produce a strong, white fabric.

By the Edo period the term *asa* referred primarily to such fabrics of ramie, and no longer bore the connotation of a coarse material for wear by common people. High quality, finely bleached ramies such as the *nara-zarashi* of Nara yielded crisp, white fabrics ideal for the unlined *katabira*, a cool and comfortable kosode-style garment for summer. See catalogue 14, 24, 34, and 35.

Asa-no-ha:
"Hemp-leaf." A purely geometric six-pointed star motif, so named for its resemblance to the shape of the hemp leaf — see the woven pattern of the *rinzu* ground of catalogue 12.

Aya:
Monochrome figured silk based on twill weaves. Figured silks called *aya* were introduced into Japan at a very early period, and the term meant figured silk in general throughout much of Japanese history. The figured silk known as *rinzu (q.v.)*, based on satin weaves, first became available in large quantities during Momoyama (1568-1615); thereafter the greater inherent design possibilities of *rinzu* led to the displacement of *aya* as a fancy figured silk, and today the term *aya* means, simply, "twill." See also *saya*.

Bōshi-shibori:
"Hat tie-dye." A version of drawn-stitch tie-dye *(nuishime-shibori, q.v.)* in which the often quite extensive stitched-off and gathered areas were given further protection from the dye bath by being wrapped into impermeable bamboo sheaths. So named because the material thus sheathed was thought to resemble a hat, perhaps the conical hat of the Dutch traders who had begun to visit Japan in Momoyama and Early Edo.

Chaya-tsuji:
A resist-dye technique of the eighteenth century, reputed to have been the proprietary development of the wealthy Chaya merchant family of Kyoto. The family was subsequently bankrupted, and the details of the technique have been lost.

In contrast to the related *yūzen* technique, in which colors were painted in by hand and then covered by resist for dyeing of the background, the fine lines of *chaya-tsuji* designs were brought out in indigo against a white background by immersion of the whole piece in the indigo vat after the entire background had been covered with starch resist, a process which might take several months. That the fine and even lines which characterize the best examples of *chaya-tsuji* could be created by such a method seems incredible today.

The dyed design was typically enhanced through restrained use of embroidery in subtle shades of red, yellow, and green, and by such techniques as *suri-hitta*. The designs, often incorporating cooling waterside or seashore motifs, were frequently inspired by songs of the past.

The use of *chaya-tsuji* dyeing was tightly controlled by the Tokugawa rulers. The method was applied primarily to the decoration of ramie *katabira* for summer court wear; see catalogue 14. It was occasionally used on silk; catalogue 15 is a particularly exquisite example on silk crepe *(chirimen)*. Late Edo techniques for the dyeing of ramie *katabira* were based upon *chaya-tsuji* but often lacked the refinement and delicacy of the 18th century examples; see catalogue 34 and 35.

Some authorities distinguish among *chaya-tsuji, chaya-zome,* and various other permutations of these terms. There is, however, no unanimity of views, and further study is required for the better understanding of this, regrettably, lost technique.

Chaya-zome:
See *chaya-tsuji*.

Chirimen:
Silk crepe. A plain weave fabric; the characteristic crinkled or crepe effect is achieved by the use of highly twisted yarns in the weft, with the direction of the twist alternating with every two successive wefts.

Because of its regular surface and rather crisp body, *chirimen* is particularly well suited as the ground for fine *yūzen* starch-resist dyeing. For examples of its use in Edo kimono see catalogue 7, 9, 16, 33, and 38.

Date-mon:
"Dandy's crest." A decorative design or device, in pattern and/or positioning resembling the *mon* or family crest, but having no heraldic significance and used purely for ornamental effect. See the butterfly medallions of catalogue 8 and the embroidered characters of catalogue 9. The elaborate crests of catalogue 42 might also be classified as *date-mon*.

Donsu:
Silk satin damask. Typically woven with dyed warp and weft yarns of different colors to produce a variegated or changeable color effect. The basic construction is a satin weave; but unlike *rinzu (q.v.)*, the material is reversible, with the pattern appearing on both sides. See catalogue 42.

Eri:
Neckband; the portion of the kimono corresponding to the collar and lapels of Western dress.

Fuji-tasuki:
"Wistaria lattice" pattern in which sprays of wistaria *(fuji)* are arranged in the *tasuki* lattice motif; see catalogue 37.

Furisode:
"Swinging sleeves." A variant of the kosode with hanging sleeves extending downward from the arms toward the waist. Despite the enlarged volume of the sleeves the furisode is regarded as a type of kosode ("small sleeves") because it retains the narrow hand openings, in contrast to the broad cuffs of the *ōsode* of classical times. First seen in the late seventeenth century (see catalogue 6), the furisode was primarily a garment for unmarried girls and entertainers; it was thought immodest for those much over nineteen. The style gained wide popularity in the Late Edo, and continues in use today. Cf. kosode, *ōsode*.

Gosho-toki:
"Views of the Imperial Palace." A Late Edo decorative style for kimono based on scenes of the gardens of the Imperial Palace in Kyoto and often incorporating pavilions, bamboo fences, ox carts, and other elements evocative of the glorious aristocratic days of Heian Japan. The style is a rich one, the entire surface being colored with abundant detail done largely in embroidery; yet the aura of refined nostalgia is reinforced by restrained execution, so that the effect is of polished elegance. See catalogue 36.

Hakama:
A full trouser-like garment of many varia-

tions, also resembling a divided skirt; formerly worn by both men and women, but now used only on highly ceremonial occasions, and primarily by men.

Hanabishi:
A stylized floral lozenge. Often it is difficult to tell whether this is a lozenge developed from a stylized flower or a floral motif developed from a lozenge. See catalogue 10.

Higaki:
"Cypress fence." A pattern resembling mats woven of strips of cypress wood for use as panels in a fence. See catalogue 42.

Hiinagata:
Catalogues of kimono design; developed simultaneously with the growth of wood-block printing as an art form in the late seventeenth and eighteenth centuries. Since fine kimono were decorated to order for the wearer, *hiinagata* served as means both for the designer to display his latest styles and for the customer to indicate her wishes to the craftsman. *Hiinagata* assumed great importance after the fires of 1657 (Edo) and 1661 (Kyoto), when there was an urgent demand for large quantities of new kimono to replace those destroyed.

Hitome-shibori:
"One-eye tie-dye," in which rows of fine knots similar to those used in *hitta* create linear elements of the design; see catalogue 20, 29, and 30.

Hitta:
A decorative tie-dye technique in which the entire area to be decorated is covered with a closely-spaced series of very fine ties. Small portions of the material are bunched up and wrapped several times with strong thread or twine. When tying is complete the material is dipped in the dye. After drying, the knots are snipped. By this method the periphery and center of each knotted bunch is dyed, but the portions constricted by the knotting thread remain undyed. See catalogue 3, 4, 11, etc.; see also the cover detail of catalogue 3.

The etymology of the word *hitta* is obscure. The technique was known in earlier (Heian) times as *meyui* ("eye-knotting"). Another, more poetic term is *kanoko* ("fawn"), used because the results resemble the dappled coat of a fawn. Some authorities distinguish between *kanoko* and *hitta*, identifying the latter as slightly coarser; by others the terms are used interchangeably. For the sake of consistency the latter term has been used exclusively in this catalogue.

Variations of the *hitta* technique include *sō-hitta* ("overall *hitta*," also called *sō-kanoko*), in which the entire surface of the material is covered with hundreds of thousands of fine *hitta* ties (catalogue 25-28); and *hitome-shibori* ("one-eye tie-dye"), in which similar fine ties are arranged in straight or curved lines to form elements of a pictorial design (catalogue 20, 29, and 30). Severe restriction of the use of *hitta* by the sumptuary regulations of the third year of Tenna (1683) led to the development of a number of imitation *hitta* techniques, including *suri-hitta (q.v.)* or *kata-hitta*; see catalogue 10. Even the severest repression, however, was unable entirely to curb this luxurious and lovely technique, which continued in use throughout the Edo and up to the present. The inherently laborious and time-consuming nature of the technique, however, prevents its very extensive use today.

Hōju:
"Jewel." The wish-fulfilling magic jewel of Buddhism, usually depicted as a "flaming" pearl, and constituting one element of the *takarazukushi (q.v.)* "myriad treasures" motif. See catalogue 31 and 32.

Ichimatsu:
Checkered pattern popularized by the actor Sanokawa Ichimatsu in the mid-eighteenth century; see catalogue 9.

Inkin:
"Impressed gold." A Heian decorative technique of Chinese origin, in which gold foil was impressed into lacquer previously applied to the surface of the material; forerunner of *surihaku (q.v.).*

Jūni-hitoe:
"Twelve single layers." The classical feminine court dress of the Heian period, consisting of multiple *ōsode* worn over a single inner kosode. The *ōsode* were dyed in differing colors, and the interplay and contrast of colors at the cuffs, neck, and hem, varied to suit the season and the individual taste of the wearer, was the primary focus of decorative interest.

Kakure-gasa:
The hat of invisibility which, together with the cloak of invisibility *(kakure-mino),* renders the wearer invisible. These charming garments are represented in the form of the sedge hat and straw rain-cape still occasion-ally encountered in rural Japan, and form important and easily identified elements in the *takarazukushi (q.v.)* "myriad treasures" motif. See catalogue 3, 31, and 32, as well as the detail of catalogue 3 on the cover (inner dark stripe on right sleeve).

Kakure-mino:
The cloak or rain-cape of invisibility; see *kakure-gasa.*

Kanoko:
"Fawn." Another, more poetic term for the dense, finely tied *hitta* tie-dye technique, because of the resemblance of the results to the dappled coat of a fawn. See *hitta.*

Karakusa:
"Chinese grass." A stylized motif of scrolling vines; see catalogue 39. The prefix *kara-* ("Chinese") is written with the character which designates the T'ang dynasty of China (618-907), a period of extensive Chinese contact with the "Western Regions" of central and western Asia, where the motif is thought to have originated; thus the parallel with the arabesque motifs of European tradition.

Katabira:
An unlined kosode-style kimono for summer wear, typically of crisp, plain-woven ramie. The finest Edo examples were decorated by the highly restricted *chaya-tsuji (q.v.)* technique; see catalogue 14 (ramie) and 15 (*chirimen* silk crepe). See also catalogue 24, 34, and 35.

Kata-hitta:
Stenciled imitation *hitta (q.v.)* tie-dye; see *suri-hitta.*

Keichō somewake:
The particolor decorative style developed in the Keichō era, 1596-1615, and popular through the mid-seventeenth century. The ground was divided into multiple interlocking panels dyed in contrasting colors, and each panel in turn was ornamented with a variety of mixed and often overlapping motifs, filling the entire ground. Techniques employed, in addition to the particolor dyeing of the ground, typically included tie-dye, embroidery, and gold leaf applique *(surihaku)*. See catalogue 2.

Kikkō:
"Tortoise-shell." The hexagon used as a design motif. See catalogue 10.

Kimono:
In the broadest sense, "clothes." More narrowly, the meaning of the word in Japanese is similar to that in English: it refers to the traditional, full-sleeved sashed outer garments worn by both men and women, as opposed to the suits and dresses of modern Western attire.

Kinran:
Gold brocade. The gold is incorporated through the use in the weft of "flat gold," very thin yarn-like strips cut from a laminate of gold foil lacquered to tough paper. The technique was developed in Sung China but was not brought to Japan until the late sixteenth century; earlier examples were all imported.

Kirigane:
"Cut gold," a later term for *zōgan (q.v.)*.

Kōkechi:
"Tie-resist." The classical Japanese term for tie-dye, now more generally called *shibori*. For the origin of the term, see catalogue 12. For an early example from the Nara period, 710-794, preserved in the Shōsō-in repository in Nara, see Minnich, figure 33. Cf. *rōkechi*, *kyōkechi*.

Koshimaki:
"Waist wrap." Originally a kosode or *uchikake (q.v.)* slipped from the shoulders and worn wrapped around the waist, suspended from the sash; later a formalized court garment worn as a train. See catalogue 31 and 32.

Kosode:
"Small sleeves." A kimono having narrow hand-openings at the ends of the sleeves, so named to distinguish it from the *ōsode* ("large sleeves"), the broad-cuffed multi-layered outer garments of classical court dress. The kosode was originally an undergarment; a similar kimono comprised the everyday wear of common people. During the feudal period of Japanese history, beginning with the Kamakura period (1185-1392), the kosode was gradually adopted as the outer garment of the samurai class as well. By Momoyama (1568-1615) and Edo (1615-1868) it had become the usual outer attire of women of all urban classes. The kosode is the forerunner of the kimono of today. See also furisode, *jūni-hitoe*, *ōsode*.

Koto:
A Japanese zither; a member of the family of long zithers with movable frets found in

China, Korea, and Vietnam as well. Roughly six feet in length, the *koto* is made of paulonia wood and has thirteen silk strings of fixed and equal length and tension; tuning is effected by means of the high, movable fret placed under each string.

Kyōkechi:
"Squeeze resist." An early resist technique in which the material was folded in two or four and placed between a pair of boards or blocks with mirror-image carved relief designs. The boards were squeezed or tied tightly together, and the dye was then poured in. The result was a two- or four-fold repeated pattern, with portions of the material constricted by the relief portions of the blocks left undyed. For an early example from the Nara period, 710-794, preserved in the Shōsō-in repository in Nara, see Minnich, figure 32. Cf. *kōkechi, rōkechi.*

Mokume-shibori:
"Wood-grain tie-dye." Achieved by gathering the material with fine parallel rows of horizontal stitching, rather like shirring. The stitches were drawn up very tightly, in order to prevent the dye from penetrating into the folds. See catalogue 6.

Mon:
Family crest; used originally for identification in battle. From the Late Edo onward family crests were commonly reserved by starch-resist in the back center and sleeves of the kimono, and often on the breasts as well. See catalogue 37-38 and 40-43. Cf. *date-mon.*

Nara-zarashi:
Fine bleached ramie produced in Nara and highly prized for use in *katabira*. See *asa, katabira.*

Noren:
The curtain hung before the door of a shop. Emblazoned with the name or mark of the shop and, often, an advertisement of the goods or services offered, the *noren* excludes prying eyes and the heat, noise and dust of the street, and serves as the sign and symbol of the business. See catalogue 38.

Nuihaku:
A decorative technique employing a combination of embroidery *(nui)* and impressed gold or silver foil *(surihaku, q.v.)*. *Nuihaku* was much used in Momoyama and Early Edo, but its importance thereafter declined as positive techniques for the application of design were supplanted by resist techniques of tie-dye and starch-resist dyeing.

Nuishime-shibori:
Drawn-stitch tie-dye, a technique in which areas to be protected from (or, conversely, exposed to) the dye bath were first carefully outlined with fine stitches. The stitches were then tightly drawn up so that the area to be protected (or exposed) was quite precisely gathered up, after which further protection could be achieved by wrapping with a bamboo sheath or other protective material. Development of such a method depended upon the availability of sufficiently supple ground materials. In use from the sixteenth century onward, it permitted far more precise results than earlier methods in which the cloth was simply bunched up and tied, and led to the development of further refinements such as

bōshi-shibori (q.v.). See catalogue 1, etc.; compare the purple clouds of catalogue 16 or the white cloud effect of catalogue 43, where simple bunching has been used, allowing the dyes to bleed.

Nume:

A lustrous, light satin-weave silk woven from raw silk and degummed in the piece. See catalogue 4. Cf. *shusu*.

Obi:

The belt or sash worn with the kimono and used to hold it closed in front — traditional Japanese dress having no buttons or other fastening devices.

In considering the evolution of kosode design in the Edo period, as illustrated in the present collection, it is essential to bear in mind that the obi formed an integral part of the costume; and that this was by no means always the wide, lavish, and formalized sash of today. Indeed, at the beginning of Edo the obi was little more than a ribbon or cord wrapped around the waist. Its evolution thereafter may perhaps best be followed in the *ukiyo-e* genre prints.

Wider obi of six or seven inches would appear to have been worn first at the end of the seventeenth century and the beginning of the eighteenth. Materials, widths, and methods of tying varied thereafter with the changes of fashion and the social position of the wearer; sumptuary regulations of varying strictness also played a part as they restricted ornamentation of the kosode and diverted attention to the sash.

The effect of the widened obi on kimono design can be seen quite clearly in some of the kosode of the Middle Edo (catalogue 9 and 10); its greatly increased importance by the end of the period is reflected in the complete absence of ornamentation in the upper part of the kimono (catalogue 37-43).

Some kimono, however, were intended to be worn unsashed, and thus no provision need be made for the interruption of the design by the obi; among such styles were the *uchikake* (catalogue 29 and 30) and the train-like *koshimaki* of the summer court (catalogue 31 and 32).

Ōsode:

"Large sleeves," the formal outer garment for women of classical Japan. So named less for the volume of the sleeves than for the broad, open cuffs, the *ōsode* was worn in multiple layers of contrasting colors; the juxtaposition of color at cuffs, neck, and hem, varied to suit the season, provided the focus of classical fashion interest. See also *jūni-hitoe*, kosode.

Ra:

An extremely light, net-like, fancy silk gauze, finer and more complex than *sha*, introduced from China at least as early as the seventh century. Several examples from the Nara period (710-794) are preserved in the *Shōsō-in* repository in Nara; but the material seems to have been little called for in the succeeding Heian period, and apparently the extremely complex weaving technique was lost until its rediscovery in the late nineteenth century.

The basic construction is a plain alternating gauze weave in which the members of each pair of warps are transposed not only with each other (as in *sha*) but also with members of the adjacent pairs on either side, such transpositions being performed after the insertion of each successive weft. The result is a very light gauze which on càsual examination looks more like a fancy knit than a woven fabric. Variations of the basic weave permit the introduction of woven motifs, of which various combinations of vertical lozenges are the most common since the weave lends itself most readily to the creation of diagonals. Cf. *ro, sha*.

Rangiku:

An often stylized floral motif, based on a combination of orchid *(ran)* and chrysanthemum *(kiku)*, and frequently used in the woven design of *rinzu* figured satin. See *rinzu*.

Rinzu:

A monochrome figured satin-weave silk imported in substantial quantities from Ming China in Momoyama and Early Edo, and subsequently woven in Japan after development of the twisting machinery required for production of the high-quality warp yarns. Though *rinzu* is often referred to as "damask," it is not a true damask since the pattern is not reversible; that is, it appears on only one side of the material. Cf. *donsu*.

A marvelously supple and lustrous material, *rinzu* was ideally suited to the sensuous drape of the kosode and to the newly developed tie-dye and resist methods which formed the basic repertoire of Edo decorative technique. Its suitability and adaptability are well attested by the fact that it is the material most frequently used in the kimono of the present collection.

Many Early Edo kosode, and doubtless some of those shown here, were made of *rinzu* imported from China. The typical woven decoration was the key-fret pattern of interconnected oblique swastikas *(saya-gata)*, on which were frequently superimposed stylized floral motifs based on the combination of orchid and chrysanthemum *(rangiku)*. This pattern can be seen most clearly in catalogue 3, 18, 22, 29, and 30; see also the cover detail of catalogue 3. Subsequently, as Japanese weavers gained more familiarity and practice with the technique, other and often more elaborate patterns were developed; see catalogue 12, 13, 39, and 41.

Ro:

A soft silk gauze woven with a combination of plain and gauze weaves, sometimes referred to as a leno weave. In contrast to *ra* and *sha* *(q.v.)*, which were woven in Japan in the Nara period (710-794) and earlier, *ro* is a comparatively later material. Softer and more pliant than *sha*, it was popular for summer kosode during the Edo period and remains in use today.

The basic construction is a plain weave with periodic horizontal or vertical rows of open "eyes" created by gauze weave. In "horizontal" *yoko-ro* the "eyes" are created by transposing the members of each pair of warps after each set of three, five, seven, or nine plain-woven wefts; in "vertical" *tate-ro* selected pairs of warps are transposed after each weft insertion, the remainder of the warps being left in plain-weave position.

116

Variations of the basic weave permit the introduction of woven patterns. See catalogue 36 and 37.

Rōkechi:

"Wax-resist" (though not written with the character for wax, *rō*). An early wax resist method analagous to the batik technique of Java, and probably originating in southern Asia. The design elements were coated with molten wax (probably a combination of waxes and resins) to prevent penetration of the dye. For an early example from the Nara period, 710-794, preserved in the Shōsō-in repository in Nara, see Minnich, figure 31. The geographical origin of the method is suggested by the exotic and tropical motifs employed.

The details of the *rōkechi* technique appear to have been forgotten after the Heian period, but it may perhaps be seen as the forerunner of the *yūzen* starch-resist dyeing of the Middle Edo and later times. Cf. *kōkechi, kyōkechi.*

Sarasa:

Historically, the multichrome calicos imported from India, Siam, and Java beginning in the late sixteenth century. The familiar chintz of the western world is of similar origin.

The Japanese word *sarasa* is thought to stem from an Indian, Javanese, or possibly Portuguese term for these fabrics, which were dyed by techniques incorporating the use of wax resist applied either by hand or by printing block, as in the batik technique still in use in Indonesia. The great popularity of these brightly colored imported goods led to the production of similar though technically inferior materials in Japan, and may well have provided some of the impetus toward the development of *yūzen (q.v.)* and related starch-resist techniques in seventeenth century Japan.

In present-day Japanese usage the term applies primarily to machine-printed calicos used largely for bedding.

Saya:

A light, monochrome figured silk introduced from China in the late sixteenth century. The word *saya* is a contraction of *sha* (gauze) and *aya* (twill); the characteristic woven pattern of *saya* was produced in twill weave on a plain ground. Similar patterns were subsequently used for the somewhat heavier *rinzu* figured satin; see *saya-gata.*

Saya-gata:

"*Saya* pattern." A geometrical pattern resembling key fretting and based on a diagonal version of the *(manji-tsunagi)* interconnected swastika motif. Originating with the light *saya* figured silks imported from China in the late sixteen century, the *saya* pattern was used frequently in the weaving of *rinzu* figured satin; see *rinzu.*

Sha:

A light, somewhat stiff silk gauze, introduced from China at a very early stage and woven throughout Japanese history down to the present day.

The basic construction is the plain gauze weave, in which the positions of each pair of warp yarns are transposed after the insertion of each successive weft. The wefts are thus tightly held by each pair of criss-crossing warps; whence the characteristic crispness of the fabric. Variations of the basic gauze weave permit the introduction of a great variety of woven patterns, some of great complexity; the material which forms the ground of catalogue 21 is a particularly fine example of *sha* gauze. Cf. *ra, ro.*

Shibori or **shibori-zome:**
Tie-dye. *Shibori* includes a great number and variety of techniques, not all of which are illustrated here. Together with starch resist dye (*yūzen-zome, chaya-tsuji, somenuki*), with which it shares the characteristic of preventing the application of color where unwanted, tie-dye served as one of the two principle elements of the flexible and spectacular Edo decorative style. See details under *bōshi-shibori, hitome-shibori, hitta, kanoko, kōkechi, mokume-shibori, nuishime-shibori, sō-hitta,* and *tsujigahana.*

Shippō:
The "seven jewels" of Buddhism, variously identified in different sources but usually including gold, silver, lapis lazuli or jade, crystal, coral, agate, and pearl; a frequent component of felicitous or auspicious designs. Perhaps because of the difficulty of concrete visualization of these materials the seven jewels are usually depicted in stylized representations of increasing abstraction, often purely geometrical shapes with round dots placed around the margins. See catalogue 31 and 32.

The *shippō-tsunagi,* a variant of the *wa-chigai* interlocked circle motif, is also linked by its name to the seven jewels theme; though the pictorial connection is difficult to grasp.

Shōchikubai:
"Pine, bamboo, and plum." A frequently encountered auspicious or felicitous motif in which the pine symbolizes long life, strength, and constancy; the bamboo, rectitude and resilience; and the plum, harmony and happiness. The combination of these three elements became almost obligatory for wedding dress. See *e.g.*, catalogue 20, 27, and 34.

Shōgun:
"Generalissimo," the title of the military rulers who, while technically subordinate to the Emperor, held effective political and military power in Japan through most of the period from the thirteenth century until 1868.

Shusu:
Plain (unfigured) satin; cf. *rinzu.* For an example of *shusu* as the material for a kimono, see the eleborately decorated furisode, catalogue 6.

Sō-hitta:
"Overall *hitta*" in which hundreds of thousands of the fine knots of the *hitta (q.v.)* technique are used to cover the entire surface of the material. See catalogue 25-28.

Sō-kanoko:
See *sō-hitta.*

Somenuki:
"Dye-omission." A resist-dye technique in which portions of the ground are covered with resist paste prior to dyeing in order to create undyed (white) lines and other design elements which might either be left untouched as parts of the design, or further embellished with embroidery, *suri-hitta,* or other decorative techniques. See, *e.g.*, catalogue 12, 33,

36, and 40. This is the technique used also to reserve family crests or *mon*; see *e.g.*, catalogue 37, 38, 40, 41, and 43.

Somewake:

"Dye-separation." A particolor dyeing technique in which the ground is separated into a number of distinct areas or panels dyed in complementary or contrasting background colors. See catalogue 1 and 24. The technique is particularly associated with the particolor style known as Keichō *somewake (q.v.)*, a style developed in the Keichō era, 1596-1615, and popular through the middle of the seventeenth century; see catalogue 2.

Surihaku:

"Rubbed foil." A decorative technique in which gold or silver leaf was rubbed or pressed into lacquer or paste brushed or stenciled onto the surface of the material. Based on the earlier *inkin (q.v.)*, the technique was much used in Momoyama, particularly in combination with embroidery *(nui)* in the combined style known as *nuihaku*. During Edo *surihaku* was frequently used in the Keichō *somewake* style *(q.v.)*, but was gradually abandoned due to the costliness of the gold, the pressure of sumptuary regulation, and the development of alternative, equally satisfying, techniques. See catalogue 3.

Suri-hitta:

Stenciled imitation tie-dye; producing the visual effect but not the characteristic surface texture of the finely knotted *hitta (q.v.)* technique. Stenciled *hitta* came into widespread use after the banning of true *hitta* by the sumptuary laws of the third year of Tenna (1683), though the technique appears actually to have been known and used somewhat prior to that time. See, *e.g.*, catalogue 10.

Suso-moyō:

"Hem design" of Late Edo, in which the ornamentation is confined to the lower portion of the skirt in reflection both of sumptuary restrictions and of the shift of fashion attention to the obi. See catalogue 40.

Takarazukushi:

The "myriad treasures" motif, a constellation of symbols of wealth, magic, and exotica, drawn from Chinese, Buddhist, South Seas, and purely Japanese sources and conveying a generally auspicious significance. The *takarazukushi* motif, standardized in that certain elements were customarily present yet variable through insertion of additional elements and flexibility in the degree of stylization, was used for the embroidered decoration of the *koshimaki* which became part of the summer uniform of palace attendants in the Late Edo; see catalogue 31 and 32. For an earlier example, see catalogue 3 and the cover detail (inner dark stripe on right sleeve). See also *hōju, kakure-gasa, shippō*, and *uchide-no-kozuchi*.

Taka-suso moyō:

"High hem design." The ornamentation covers the entire skirt of the kimono below the obi but does not extend into the upper portion. A formal variant of the hem design *(suso-moyō, q.v.)*; see catalogue 37.

Tasuki:

A lattice pattern of crossed diagonal lines, so named after the cord used to bind up the sleeves of the farmer's or working man or woman's kimono, which forms an oblique cross over the back.

Tsujigahana:
A decorative technique and style based on the combination of tie-dye with hand-drawn detailing. The tie-dye was often bunched rather than sewn, with indistinct borders which contrasted with the precision of the hand-done details. The pigments used and the passage of time have given presently extant examples a lovely washed patina.

First developed in Muromachi (1392-1568) *tsujigahana* became the characteristic decorative style of Momoyama (1568-1615), with which it is closely identified. During Edo it was supplanted by newer tie-dye and resist techniques, made possible in part by the appearance of a more supple medium in the form of *rinzu* figured satin. The present collection accordingly includes no examples of pure *tsujigahana*, though the design of catalogue 1 draws much from the *tsujigahana* tradition.

The etymology of the term *tsujigahana* is both obscure and controversial.

Uchide-no-kozuchi:
The mallet of fortune, which pours forth riches with every shake; a counterpart of the cornucopia or Aladdin's lamp. Represented with a shortened handle which protrudes on both sides of the head, and perhaps not immediately identifiable as a mallet, the *uchide-no-kozuchi* is an element of the *taka-razukushi (q.v.)* "myriad treasure" motif. See catalogue 31 and 32.

Uchikake:
An over-kimono or cloak worn over the kimono and obi on formal or ceremonious occasions and clasped in front by the hands, without the use of a sash. The style originated in the Kamakura period, 1185-1392, when attractively decorated kosode were worn in the manner described. In Edo and modern usage the term refers specifically to lavish and elaborate kosode or furisode with wadded trailing hems expressly designed to be so worn; however any kosode or furisode with an appropriately decorative design might be so worn. See catalogue 29 and 30.

Ukiyo-e:
"Pictures of the fleeting (literally, 'floating') world." The new genre of painting and wood-block prints developed by and for the prosperous bourgeoise society of Edo Japan. The genre was at first confined to such topical subject matter as famous actors and beautiful women, but later expanded to include also urban scenes and landscapes. *Ukiyo-e* prints serve as an important source of information on contemporary fashion and costume design.

Wa-chigai:
A geometric motif consisting of interlocking or overlapping circles; see catalogue 39.

Yabure wa-chigai:
"Broken *wa-chigai*," a lattice-like motif consisting of fragments of the *wa-chigai* pattern of interlocking circles. See catalogue 43.

Yogi:
"Night clothing." Not actually an item of apparel but rather a sleeved coverlet, resembling a heavily padded kimono in cut and construction but intended to be thrown over the bedding rather than worn. See catalogue 19.

Yukiwa:

"Snow ring." The term is also found translated as "snowflake ring," "snow disk," "snow crystal," etc. A highly stylized representation of snow, the *yukiwa* is a notched circular ring or disk. The number of notches is often, but not always, six. See catalogue 3, and cover detail, where only the lower left quarter of the pattern is represented.

Yūzen-zome:

The marvelously flexible multichrome starch-resist dyeing process perfected during the Middle Edo period and still in use today.

In one of many variations the outlines of the design are first drawn in by hand, using a resist paste made from glutinous rice applied with a pointed stick. The colors are then painted in and fixed, after which the design is entirely covered by resist and the material dyed to obtain the background color. The resist is then removed by rinsing in a fast-running stream. In a later, more mechanical variation the resist is applied by stencil.

For the background and development of Edo *yūzen* see the Introduction. Perhaps the earliest Japanese ancestor of *yūzen* resist dyeing was the *rōkechi* wax resist of the Nara period, and added stimulus for the development of resist techniques may well have been provided by the popularity of the *sarasa* chintz imported from India and Siam from the late sixteenth century onward; foreign *sarasa* was also dyed in part by wax resist.

The use of starch as a resist material, however, was not entirely unknown in pre-Edo Japan. The basic starch-resist technique can be traced back to Muromachi (1392-1568), and examples survive from Momoyama (1568-1615). See Osaka shiritsu bijutsukan, comp., *Sekai no senshoku* (1973; unpaginated: see text section on Edo textile techniques).

Nonetheless it was not until the Middle Edo that the use of starch resist was fully developed and perfected in the *yūzen* technique. Particularly exquisite examples of its use in Middle and Late Edo are catalogue 7, 9, 16, and 38.

Zōgan:

"Inlay." A Heian period decorative technique in which designs cut from gold foil were affixed to the surface of cloth with lacquer.

Joseph S. Hayes, Jr.

SELECTED BIBLIOGRAPHY

WORKS IN ENGLISH

CIBA Limited, ed. "Japanese Resist-dyeing Techniques." *CIBA Review*, 1967/4. Basle: CIBA, 1967.

Dunn, Charles J. *Everyday Life in Traditional Japan*. Tokyo: Tuttle, 1972.

Emery, Irene. *The Primary Structures of Fabrics: An Illustrated Classification.* Washington, D.C.: The Textile Museum, 1966.

Gunsaulus, Helen C. *Japanese Textiles.* Privately printed for the Japan Society of New York, 1941.

Japan Textile Color Design Center. *Textile Designs of Japan*. 3 vols. Osaka: Japan Textile Color Design Center, 1959-1961.

Mailey, Jean. "Four Hundred Winters… Four Hundred Springs…". *The Metropolitan Museum of Art Bulletin,* December 1959.

Minnich, Helen Benton, in collaboration with Shojiro Nomura. *Japanese Costume: And the Makers of Its Elegant Tradition.* Rutland, Vermont and Tokyo, Japan: Charles E. Tuttle Co., 1963.

Mizoguchi, Saburō. *Design Motifs.* Translated and adapted by Louise Allison Cort. Arts of Japan, vol. 1. New York and Tokyo: Weatherhill, Shibundo, 1973.

Noma, Seiroku. *Japanese Costume and Textile Arts.* Translated by Armins Nikovskis. The Heibonsha Survey of Japanese Art, vol. 16. New York and Tokyo: Weatherhill, Heibonsha, 1974.

Okada, Yuzuru, and Yamanobe, Tomoyuki. *Textiles and Lacquer.* Translated by Charles S. Terry. Pageant of Japanese Art, vol. 5. Tokyo: Tōto Shuppan Company, 1953 (deluxe edition) and 1958 (popular edition).

Parish, H. Carroll. "The Mon: Japanese Equivalent of the European Coat-of-Arms." *The Augustan*, vol. 14, no. 3 (May-June 1971), pp. 122-137.

Simmons, Pauline. "Artist Designers of the Tokugawa Period." *The Metropolitan Museum of Art Bulletin*, February 1956.

Tatsumura, Heizo. "Favorite Colors with the Change of Time." *Palette*, no. 29 (1968).

Yamanobe, Tomoyuki. *Textiles*. English adaptation by Lynn Katoh. Arts and Crafts of Japan, no. 2. Rutland, Vermont and Tokyo, Japan: Tuttle, 1957.

_____. "Textiles." In *Decorative Arts of Japan*, edited by Chisaburoh F. Yamada, pp. 203-235. Tokyo: Kodansha International, 1964.

_____. "Japanese Theatrical Costume and its Color Symbolism." *Palette*, no. 29 (1968).

WORKS IN JAPANESE AND ENGLISH

Kyoto kokuritsu hakubutsukan (Kyoto National Museum), comp. *Tokubetsu tenrankai: Kyō no senshoku-bi: Momoyama kara Edo made (Special Exhibition: Beauty of Textile Arts in Kyoto: 16th through 19th Centuries.)* Kyoto: Kyoto shōkō kaigisho (Kyoto Chamber of Commerce and Industry), 1975.

Tokyo kokuritsu hakubutsukan (Tokyo National Museum). *Tokubetsu-ten: 'Nihon no senshoku' (Special Exhibition: Japanese Textile Arts)*. Tokyo: Tokyo kokuritsu hakubutsukan (Tokyo National Museum), 1973.

_____. *Nihon no senshoku (Japanese Textile Arts)*. Tokyo: Tokyo kokuritsu hakubutsukan (Tokyo National Museum), 1974.

WORKS IN JAPANESE

I-seikatsu kenkyūkai (Society for the Study of Clothing Habits). *Dentō kōgei: Senshoku-hen (Traditional Industrial Arts: Dyeing and Weaving)*. 18 vols. Tokyo: I-seikatsu kenkyūkai, 1973.

Kamiya Eiko. *Kosode*. Nihon no bijutsu (Arts of Japan), no. 67. Tokyo: Shibun-dō, 1971.

Kanebō kabushiki kaisha, Ishō kenkyū-bu (Kanebo, Ltd., Design Research Department), comp. *Kanebō korekushon: Nihon no senshoku (The Kanebo Collection: Dyeing and Weaving of Japan)*. Kyoto: Kōrinsha, 1974-1975.

Nishimura Hyōbu. *Orimono (Textiles)*. Nihon no bijutsu (Arts of Japan), no. 12. Tokyo: Shibun-dō, 1971.

_____. Yamanobe Tomoyuki; Kitamura Tetsurō; Kamiya Eiko; *et al. Nihon senshoku-geijutsu sōsho (Library of the Dyeing and Weaving Arts of Japan)*. 10 vols. Tokyo and Kyoto: Unsō-dō, 1971-1976.

Osaka shiritsu bijutsukan (Osaka Municipal Museum of Art), comp. *Sekai no senshoku (Dyeing and Weaving of the World)*. Osaka: Kanebō, 1973.

Tokyo kokuritsu hakubutsukan (Tokyo National Museum). *Nihon fukushoku bijutsuten mokuroku (Catalogue of the Exhibition of the Arts of Japanese Dress and Ornamentation)*. Tokyo: Tokyo bijutsu, 1972.

Yamanobe Tomoyuki and Kitamura Tetsurō. *Kosode*. 2 vols. Tokyo: San-ichi shobō, 1967.

_____. *Some (Dyeing)*. Nihon no bijutsu (Arts of Japan), no. 7. Tokyo: Shibun-dō, 1971.

FRIENDS OF JAPAN HOUSE GALLERY

*Mrs. Vincent Astor
*Mr. and Mrs. Douglas Auchincloss
 Mrs. Harold L. Bache
*Mr. and Mrs. Armand P. Bartos
*Mr. Joe Brotherton
*Mrs. Jackson Burke
*Dr. and Mrs. Walter A. Compton
*Mrs. Cornelius Crane
 Mr. and Mrs. Edgar M. Cullman, Jr.
 Mr. and Mrs. Lewis B. Cullman
 Mr. and Mrs. Richard M. Danziger
*Mr. and Mrs. C. Douglas Dillon
*Mr. and Mrs. Peter F. Drucker
 Mrs. Frederick L. Ehrman
 Mrs. Richard Ellis
*Mr. and Mrs. Myron S. Falk, Jr.
*Mr. and Mrs. Charles A. Greenfield
*Mr. Louis W. Hill, Jr.
*Mr. and Mrs. William H. Johnstone
*Ms. Margot P. Kneeland

*Mr. Yale Kneeland III
 Mrs. H. Irgens Larsen
*Mrs. Louis V. Ledoux
*Mr. and Mrs. Henry A. Loeb
 Mr. and Mrs. Richard D. Lombard
*Mr. Stanley J. Love
 Mr. and Mrs. C. Richard MacGrath
 The Edward John Noble Foundation
*Mr. and Mrs. S. Morris Nomura
*Mr. and Mrs. Joe D. Price
*Mrs. John D. Rockefeller 3rd
*Mrs. Aye Simon
 Mr. Irwin M. Stelzer
*Mr. and Mrs. Donald B. Straus
*Mrs. Arnold L. van Ameringen
 Mr. Henry P. van Ameringen
*Mrs. Lila Acheson Wallace
*Mr. Richard W. Weatherhead
*Ms. Lucia Woods

*Founder

OFFICERS OF JAPAN SOCIETY, INC.

Mr. John D. Rockefeller 3rd, Chairman of the Board
Mrs. Jackson Burke, Vice Chairman of the Board
Mr. James M. Voss, Vice Chairman of the Board
Mr. Tatsuro Goto, Vice Chairman of the Board
Mr. Isaac Shapiro, President
Mr. Edgar B. Young, Vice President
Mr. Charles R. Stevens, Secretary
Mr. Tristan E. Beplat, Treasurer
Mr. David MacEachron, Executive Director

ADVISORY COMMITTEE ON ARTS

Dr. Richard F. Brown
Mr. Richard S. Cleveland
Mr. Arthur Drexler
Dr. Calvin L. French
Dr. Sherman E. Lee
Mr. William S. Lieberman
Dr. Miyeko Murase
Dr. John Rosenfield
Dr. Harold P. Stern
Mr. Henry Trubner

COMMITTEE ON CARE AND HANDLING

Mr. Abe Mitsuhiro
Mr. Iguchi Yashuhiro
Mr. Sugiura Takashi

Cover Illustration: Catalogue 3
Detail of upper right portion
Kosode with chrysanthemums and snowflake ring
Tie-dye *(hitta)*, embroidery, and gold leaf *(surihaku)*
White figured satin *(rinzu)*
Early Edo; 145.0 cm x 61.5 cm

Catalogue designed by Kiyoshi Kanai, New York
Photographs by Kōrinsha Printing Co., Ltd., Kyoto, Japan
Composition by Franklin Typographers, Inc., New York
Printed by Kōrinsha Printing Co., Ltd., Kyoto, Japan